The Making of
JAMES CLAVELL'S
SHŌGUN

A DELTA BOOK

A DELTA BOOK

Published by
Dell Publishing Co., Inc.
1 Dag Hammarskjold Plaza
New York, New York 10017

Published by arrangement with The Van Ness Organization:
3696 Mandeville Canyon Road, Los Angeles, CA 90049
Editorial: Elizabeth Barks and Paul Bernstein
Art Direction and Design: Kadi Karist Tint
Production: Project Publishing & Design
Production Management: Author/Publisher Services:
1512 Eleventh St., Santa Monica, CA 90401

Photographs courtesy of Paramount Pictures Corporation.

Delta ® TM 755118, Dell Publishing Co., Inc.

ISBN: 0-440-55709-7

Printed in the United States of America
First printing—September 1980

Acknowledgments

In addition to those interviewed for THE MAKING OF SHŌGUN, we wish to thank the following people, without whose help and support this book would not have been possible:

April and James Clavell
Elizabeth Barks
Paul Bernstein
Arlene Castiglione
Curt Cowan
Bob and Maggie Dawson
Ruth Engelhardt
Kerry Feltham
Eric and Maureen Lasher
Mark Lofstrom
Valerie Nelson
Dan Richland
Miiko Taka
Kadi Karist Tint
Richard J. Winters

and a special thanks to Maria Esnet Villada de Franco.

Production Credits for
James Clavell's
SHŌGUN

Executive Producer	James Clavell	Music Composed and	
Director of		Conducted by	Maurice Jarre
Photography	Andrew Laszlo, A.S.C.	Production Executive	Frank Cardea
Production Designer	Joseph R. Jennings	From the Novel by	James Clavell
Film Editors	James T. Heckert	Written for Television and	
	Bill Luciano	Produced by	Eric Bercovici
	Donald R. Rode	Directed by	Jerry London
	Benjamin A. Weissman		
	Jerry Young		

Sound Mixer	John Glascock	Unit Production Managers	Ben Chapman
Stunt Coordinator	Glenn Wilder		Wally Worsley
Production Accountant	Don Henry	1st Assistant Directors	Charles Ziarko
Auditor	J. Steven Hollander		Phil Cook
Property Master	Marty Wunderlich	"Blackthorne's Shanty" Words	
Painter	Ed Charnock	and Music by	Eric Bercovici
Program Assistant	Chiho Adachi	Set Decorator	Tom Pedigo
Assistant to Eric Bercovici	Anna Mills	Assistant Production Manager	Chris Bartlett
Assistant to James Clavell	Valerie Nelson	Construction Coordinator	Al DeGaetano
Main Title by Phil Norman & Westheimer Co.		Special Effects	Robert Dawson
Recorded by	Glen Glenn Sound	Sound Editor	Howard Beals
Lenses and Panaflex Camera by Panavision®		Music Editor	John LaSalandra
Casting by	Maude Spector	Camera Operator	Chuy Elizondo
	Tatsuhiko Kuroiwa	Gaffer	Sal Orefice
Special Consultant	Fred Ishimoto	Key Grips	Ken Johnston
Associate Producers	Kerry Feltham		Vern Matthews
	Ben Chapman	Dialogue Director	Luca Bercovici
		Script Supervisor	Larry K. Johnson

JAPANESE CREW

Art Director	Yoshinobu Nishioka	Set Decorator	Shoichi Yasuda
Costume Designer	Shin Nishida	Make-up	Masato Abe
Unit Production Managers	Shinji Nakagawa	Wardrobe	Toshiaki Manki
	Kazuo Shizukawa	Construction Department	Hideo Yoshioka
	Keisuke Shinoda	Script Supervisor	Chiyo Miyakoshi
Advisor to Jerry London	Umeo Minamino	Stunt Coordinator	Shinpachi Miyama
Assistant Director	Masahiko Okumura		

The Cast of
James Clavell's
SHŌGUN

Blackthorne	Richard Chamberlain	Specz	Morgan Sheppard
Toranaga	Toshiro Mifune	Muraji	Seiji Miyaguchi
Mariko	Yoko Shimada	Hiromatsu	Toru Abe
Yabu	Frankie Sakai	Kiku	Mika Kitagawa
Father dell'Aqua	Alan Badel	Naga	Shin Takuma
Friar Domingo	Michael Hordern	Jirobei	Hyoei Enoki
Father Alvito	Damien Thomas	Galley Captain	Hiroshi Hasegawa
Rodrigues	John Rhys-Davies	Old Gardener	Akira Sera
Ferriera	Vladek Sheybal	Kiri	Miiko Taka
Vinck	George Innes	Yoshinaka	Rinichi Yamamoto
Father Sebastio	Leon Lissek	Sazuko	Yuko Kada
Omi	Yuki Meguro	Sono	Midori Takei
Ishido	Nobuo Kaneko	Rako	Ai Matsubara
Buntaro	Hideo Takamatsu	Asa	Yumiko Morishita
Fujiko	Hiromi Senno	Brother Michael	Masumi Okada
Pieterzoon	Edward Peel	Zataki	Yosuke Natsuki
Maetsukker	Eric Richard	Urano	Takeshi Ohbayashi
Roper	Steve Ubels	Gyoko	Yoshie Kitsuda
Croocq	Stewart MacKenzie	Suga	Masashi Ebara
Ginsel	John Carney	Genjiko	Setsuko Sekine
Salamon	Ian Jentle	Lady Ochiba	Atsuko Sano
Spillbergen	Neil McCarthy		

Filmed entirely on location in Japan.
Permission to film Himeji Castle courtesy of Himeji City, Japan.
The vessel the Golden Hinde was photographed in this production.

Foreword
by James Clavell

This book tells the story of the making of *Shōgun*, converting the novel from book form to film form. But it tells only part of the story. The whole story cannot be told because then you would have to have the input of half a thousand others—Americans, Japanese, and Europeans spread throughout the earth; the input of our Japanese partners Matsuoko of Toho, Miura of TV Asahi, Newbigging of Jardine's, and Uemura of Tohokushinsha; publishers like Helen Meyer, Michael Attenborough, Ross Claiborne, Carl Tobey; financiers, deal makers, agents—the unknown NBC executives who actually *decided* and pressed the button to initiate the whole wonderful adventure—the Paramount brass, Barry Diller, Michael Eisner and Gary Nardino, who allowed us to enter the lists—men like Michael Ovitz, who made the deal between NBC and Paramount and myself, and held the deal together when doom walked the stars.

Lots of doom walks lots of stars in our business.

All those people have part of the story to tell, and then there are the historical figures who became patterns for me: Will Adams, English navigator, who really did go to Japan in 1600 and became a samurai; Nobunaga, Hideyoshi, and Tokugawa, the giants of those days in Japan, who were real people and walked the earth like titans—living, loving, killing, and creating history.

For me, this book is the manifestation of a miracle.

It is a miracle that *Shōgun* came to pass as a novel, let alone twelve hours for NBC and a motion picture as well. It's miraculous that my Blackthorne has come to life, and Toranaga and Mariko and all the others so...beautifully. Oh, yes, it is indeed miraculous.

The essence of any film is the screenplay, and when at the eleventh hour the stuff was really hitting the fan—and in our business it hits the fan most every day—I girded my loins and petitioned heaven. Heaven sent me Eric Bercovici, screenwriter and subsequently producer. Together we chose Jerry London to direct and together we cast the film. For our principals, Richard Chamberlain, Toshiro Mifune, and Yoko Shimada, I have nothing but praise. They gave of themselves limitlessly. And so did all the others: Frankie Sakai, Damien Thomas, Yuki Meguro, and the hundreds in the cast; the technicians, American and Japanese—they, too, gave more than they had ever given before, freely. I thank them.

Curiously—I don't really understand why—I believe this is the essence of the *Shōgun* project: the almost magical obsessive giving and wish of everyone concerned for it to succeed.

In the end you, the public, will be the judge of that. But let it be said openly for everyone who had any part in the making of *Shōgun*, big, small, or tiny, that we've all tried to do the best we could for you....

Contents

Page to Screen

The 16th century warship, far from home, bobbed and rolled on the rough waters off Japan. Finally, after 55 days at sea, land was sighted. "All hands on deck," the captain cried. Sixteen bedraggled hands squinted into the rain for a glimpse of their destination. Awaiting them was the Land of the Gods, a land of samurai and seppuku, of honor and intrigue, of great beauty and unexpected danger.

As the three-masted Erasmus sailed into Yokohama, a bearded captain with a smart white uniform and navy blue cap gestured towards the shore. A flag bearing 13 red and white stripes and 50 stars on a blue background was unfurled. On the shore, a brass band, dressed in red, struck up a rousing, Western tune. A child in overalls waved. Cameras and balloons went off. A small motor-boat zipped out to escort the crew through a waiting crowd of hand-shakers and autograph-seekers.

*The Golden Hinde
as the Erasmus.*

Ready to embark.

The Erasmus had arrived—for the second time. The first time, in a novel called *Shōgun*, it came into an unknown land where its pilot, John Blackthorne, was to discover the often superior ways of the Orient. The second time, some 400 years later, another Erasmus (actually the Golden Hinde, on loan from its owners in San Francisco) arrived to begin filming the massive story of Blackthorne and his crew.

This time, the Erasmus had it a bit easier. It came, with modern conveniences, to a land where the influence of the West had already been felt. It came to join some 30 Americans in a nine-month filmmaking project, a project in which they would count on the assistance of several hundred Japanese actors, technicians, and researchers. It came to tell a Western story from a Western perspective, with the goal of increasing understanding between two cultures.

But while this century's voyage of the Erasmus may not compare with Blackthorne's fictional undertaking, it did have its epic proportions. Three quarters of a million feet of film were shot, at a cost of $22 million. Sets and costumes alone ran more than $3 million. The entire village of Anjiro, the imaginary site where Blackthorne first landed, was constructed from scratch in a quiet cove near Nagashima. The script, by Eric Bercovici, involved 1,062 scenes and 2,749 camera set-ups.

The Golden Hinde leaving San Francisco Bay.

And the complications were epic as well. Problems in dealing with a different culture and language proved even greater than expected, and led to impasses which were frustrating in the moment but instructive and even comic in retrospect. Acts of God—a typhoon that destroyed the sets of Anjiro, an earthquake scene that went wrong and buried the special effects director alive, constant struggles with the weather—occasionally made the Western crew wonder if they, like Blackthorne, might be spending the rest of their lives in Japan.

‡ ‡ ‡

The story of Blackthorne has become a familiar one to the 4 million readers of the novel *Shōgun*, but until 10 years ago it was but a vague image in the mind of author James Clavell. It was in his daughter's history book, in fact, that Clavell's idea originated. A single line was enough to inspire 1210 pages of novel. "In 1600," it said simply, "an Englishman went to Japan and became a samurai."

That Englishman was Will Adams, the first and only foreigner ever to become a Japanese samurai. Like Blackthorne, he was pilot major of a Dutch fleet with five ships. Like Blackthorne, he set out to circumnavigate the globe and wound up in Japan. In Japan, he found himself up against England's enemies, the Portuguese and the Jesuits, who already had a strong foothold there. By his wits and his good fortune, Will Adams was able to gain the confidence of Ieyasu Tokugawa, a legendary figure who unified several unwieldy factions into one nation under his rule as Japan's first Shōgun. And because Adams knew so much that could help them, the Japanese burned his ship to keep him from going home.

Did Clavell just plug in the names then—John Blackthorne for Will Adams, Toranaga for Ieyasu Tokugawa, Nakamura for Hideyoski Toyotomi, the taiko? No, says Clavell. "I'm a storyteller, not an historian."

With *Shōgun*, Clavell was writing an historical novel which he tried to keep as accurate as possible—while still staying in the realm of fiction. "I've found that if you can discover what really happened, it's usually more interesting than anything you can invent yourself," he says. "A large portion of

Opposite page: London, Clavell, and Bercovici aboard the Golden Hinde.

Rodrigues and Blackthorne sail for Osaka.

The *Erasmus,* moored in the Land of the Gods.

Left:
Sebastio orders the samurai to attack.

Below:
A samurai holds Blackthorne at swordpoint.

Bottom:
Omi's first meeting with Blackthorne.

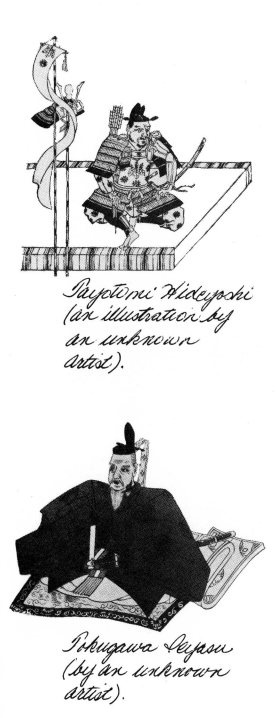

Toyotomi Hideyoshi
(an illustration by
an unknown
artist).

Tokugawa Ieyasu
(by an unknown
artist).

Shōgun is historically accurate. But I've not been there, you've not been there, and the people who wrote the histories were only reporting *their* version. And their version is biased. So who the hell knows *what* really happened? I have reconstructed as accurately as I can the sort of man that Will Adams was. But Blackthorne is *not* Will Adams. How dare I be so pretentious?"

In the novelizing process, Clavell took certain scenes from history and reworked them for dramatic effect. For example, in one history book he found a report of Tokugawa and Hideyoshi, sealing a bargain by urinating together and mixing their urine. The upshot of the deal was to unite against the then occupants of the Kwanto, a valuable section of eastern Japan that produces the best rice crops. In the novel, Clavell moved the scene to the top of a castle, and changed the nature of the bargain.

In the novel, Clavell gave the name Rodrigues to a Portuguese pilot. His source for the name was another Rodrigues, a Jesuit priest who lived from 1561 to 1633 and became the most influential European in Japan—a confidant to Japan's supreme ruler, Hideyoshi, and to his successor, Tokugawa. The real-life Rodrigues provided a model for the Jesuit priests in *Shōgun*. Both fictional and real-life Jesuits were interpreters, authors of the first Japanese grammar book, and active participants in the silk trade between Japan and China.

"As far as historical accuracy goes," says the author, "part of it is obviously intuitive. But much of it is based on a copious bibliography, including everything I could find on Japan and Japanese thinking. There are several books on the life of Hideyoshi Toyotomi (the taiko), another book on Tokugawa, and the famous *Book of Tea*, written by a Japanese in English. You have to plough through dozens upon dozens of pieces of information to find one piece that sparks you. And you must capture the attitude. By reading and listening to people, you can hopefully discover something about their mores. I tried to put those Japanese mores into a Western context in fictional terms."

The story of Will Adams also gives us the ending of Blackthorne's story. The ship that Blackthorne is building at the

Right:
Damien Thomas
as Father Alvito.

Left:
John Rhys-Davies
as Rodrigues.

end of *Shōgun*—Will Adams built one, too, but Tokugawa took it away from him and gave it to the Governor General of the Philippines. Adams was then sent to Nagasaki, where all the Portuguese in Japan had been confined, and put to work with a large salary as Inspector General of the forces there. When Adams asked about his ship, he was told simply that it would not be convenient for him to leave Japan at that particular time. Adams later was allowed to travel with Japanese vessels as far as Siam and China, on business for Tokugawa. The Japanese at that time were not permitted to land in China, because of their reputation for excessive belligerence, so intermediaries like Adams and the Jesuits conducted the trade between the two

countries. Adams left a log of those journeys and wrote letters home, five of which are now in the British Museum.

"But I *repeat*," says Clavell, "*Shōgun* is not the story of Will Adams. It is the story of an Englishman who went to Japan and became a samurai."

It is also the story of a Westerner who was made a prisoner of the Japanese and had every reason to hate them, but who gradually was seduced by their culture. Blackthorne's story is, in that respect, the story of Clavell as well. At the age of 18, as an officer in the World War II Royal Artillery, Clavell was taken prisoner by the Japanese and kept for three and a half years at a large prison camp near Singapore. There, he says, the prisoners lived like "rubber planters"; 14 out of every 15 died.

How, then, did prisoner Clavell come to be an admirer of his captors? "I didn't hate them for doing the things that others hated them for, because I began to understand them. Their code was that we had lost honor because we had allowed ourselves to be captured," he says.

But it was a long time before he could speak openly about his experiences in the prison camp. His first novel, *King Rat*, written in the early sixties about the camp, was the catharsis he needed. "After that, I could write a passionately pro-Japanese thing and be gentle with a great deal of understanding about the Japanese. I can't explain it myself either. I usually say, 'Well, I was Japanese in a previous life.' "

‡   ‡   ‡

For a novel that was to have such huge success, the moviemakers had surprisingly little enthusiasm at first. Apparently, they were scared off by the weight of the book. "Heads of studios, when the book was in galley form or even in manuscript form, looked at the amounts of paper and they said it couldn't be done," recalls Clavell. "Few people read it. Those that did didn't understand the simplicity of how it could be done. 'Where's the market for it?' they asked.

"For a long time I had much difficulty explaining to them that this is a simple story of a man who goes to Japan, becomes a samurai, falls in love with a beautiful lady, and loses

Opposite page: James Clavell and director Jerry London.

Blackthorne confesses his feelings for Mariko.

her. It's *Madam Butterfly*. It's a very simple story, even though it's told on many levels as a book.''

Finally, in exasperation, he said, "Christ, *I* know how to do it. Give me the money and *I'll* do it.''

He wasn't just talking. While Clavell is best known as a novelist, he also has impressive credits as a screenwriter, as a producer, and as a director. He served as all three for *To Sir, With Love* and *The Last Valley*. In fact, he has been in film longer than he has been in novels. When he came to America after the war, he wanted to become a director. He went around knocking on doors at the studios but, like so many other would-be filmmakers, got no response. So he began to write screenplays. Rather than continue with the door-to-door route that had proven so unsuccessful, he concocted a plan worthy of a future novelist. He announced to anyone willing to listen that he had discovered a brilliant new screenwriter whose latest screenplay he had agreed to direct. The brilliant new screenwriter was none other than Clavell himself, writing under a pseudonym. His efforts eventually led to the sale of his first screenplay, for that late-night horror movie *The Fly*. He went on to write *The Great Escape*, *633 Squadron*, and *The Satan Bug*, and to adapt a number of novels to film. His first novel came about only because of a screenwriters' strike in the early sixties; during the lull, he wrote *King Rat*.

So when he found the studios unresponsive on the subject of *Shōgun*, he had the tools and credentials to do it himself. He hired an Academy Award-winning writer, Robert Bolt, and he signed on Richard Attenborough as producer.

Then came *Roots*, and *Roots* changed everything, for it was the first production to prove the viability of the long form on television. It was the answer to *Shōgun's* problems. Within weeks, Clavell was on the phone to his agent, asking, "Look, what about the long form?" NBC, convinced by *Roots*, took an option on *Shōgun* and paid for hiring a new writer and producer. They told Clavell they would close the deal if he could come to an agreement with one of four studios they suggested to produce the film. Paramount, who had been interested in the original film version, came through. The plans for the first film were junked, and work started on a 12-hour "maxi-series" for television which would also be cut as a two-and-a-half-hour version for theatrical release.

"*Roots* unlocked it," says Clavell. "*Roots* is the key. And if *Roots* is the key, I'm hoping that *Shōgun* will be the cement in a new attitude towards TV. Because this film is not made for television. It is made in the best possible way, on film, irrespective of the size of the screen. It's pretentious to say it will 'upgrade' or 'downgrade' television, but I think it will create a standard that other people have to match, and they will find it rather hard to do."

Because of his track record in film, Clavell was able to retain the kind of creative control over the project that other authors understandably would envy. His title was "executive producer," which can mean anything from general overseer to ultimate boss. Clavell, in his first attempt at television and his first attempt at being an executive producer, saw the job as something on the order of a general commanding his troops. And if Clavell was the commanding general, an Eisenhower perhaps, he saw his producer-screenwriter Eric Bercovici as a Patton, a strong, tough field general who could be trusted to implement the overall plan.

Paramount's arrangement called for three Japanese partners—Toho Studios, Asahi television network, and Jardine-Mathieson, a large Hong Kong trading company. It was strictly a financial arrangement. The Japanese would get rights to show a two-and-a-half-hour theatrical version of *Shōgun*. The creative control rested with Clavell.

Clavell insisted that all of *Shōgun* be filmed in Japan. To a studio executive who, early on, suggested filming on location in England and Sardinia, Clavell answered promptly and forcefully, "That's manure. You can't do that. Not if you want to make *Shōgun*. If you want to make something else, that's your business. But if it's *Shōgun* you are making, absolutely no."

Filming on location in Japan would be the factor that gave *Shōgun* as a film its undeniable authenticity. But it would also present more problems than anyone imagined.

James Clavell visiting the set.

Above:
Ginsel, Blackthorne,
and Salamon in
the pit.

Right:
Blackthorne defies
Omi.

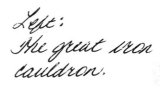

Preparing for
Blackthorne's first
Japanese bath.

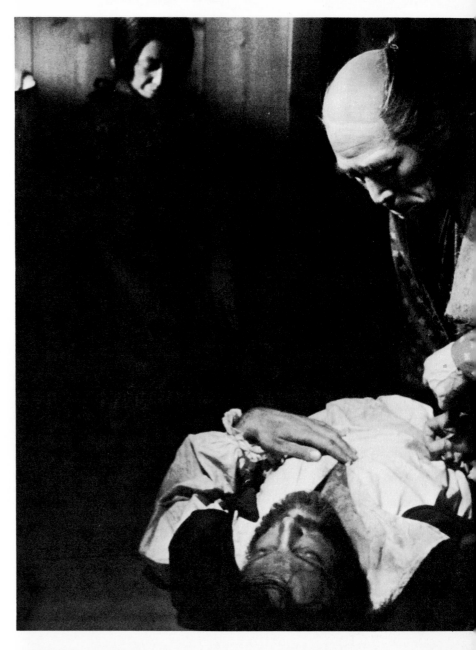

Soaped, scrubbed,
and relaxed.

Above:
A clean Englishman!

Left:
Children of Anjiro.

Below:
Omi and Sebastio
take Blackthorne to
Hiromatsu.

Bottom:
The galley at the
jetty.

If you were to read the 400,000 words of *Shōgun*, the novel, aloud at the rate of 100 words a minute, it would take you a little more than 66 hours, or almost three days, to finish. Imagine, then, the task that confronted writer-producer Eric Bercovici in reducing the novel to what in dramatic terms is still an exceptionally long production—12 hours. He had experience with other versions of the long form in television, notably the Watergate drama *Washington: Behind Closed Doors*.

But *Shōgun* was a more complicated matter. Much of the novel's appeal lies in the complicated political intrigue, which often takes place without Blackthorne's knowledge, and the cumulative effect of a detailed exposure to 16th century Japanese culture. It would be impossible to get all of that into any film, even a 12-hour one. In their first meeting, Clavell simplified matters for Bercovici. "It's a love story," he told the screenwriter. "It's the story of a man who goes to Japan, becomes a samurai, and falls in love."

Clavell figured that, in translating his story to film, they would have to center on Blackthorne, Mariko, and Toranaga. Ishido, Toranaga's political rival, would come in, but as a smaller character than in the book. Ochiba would be there, too, but in a still smaller role. The politics would be there, the heir would be there, the flavor of an alien world would be there, but the story on film was to be basically an old and universal one: boy meets girl, boy wins girl, boy loses girl.

When Bercovici came to the project in February of 1979, the first task he set for himself was to read *Shōgun* four times cover to cover. If he were to choose what would be dropped and what would be retained, he thought, it was imperative that he know the book better than anyone else. After studying the book carefully, he came up with the approach that was to make or break the screen *Shōgun*.

The plan was simple: The entire story would be told through Blackthorne's eyes. What he saw, we saw. What he heard, we heard. What he understood, we understood. And what he did not understand, we did not understand. The Japanese were to speak Japanese—no subtitles, no dubbing, no accents. And by the end, a few words of Japanese vocabulary would be understandable to the audience.

Eric Bercovici and James Clavell.

To see how it would work, Clavell took a paperback copy of the book, went through it page by page, and physically ripped out anything that would have to be eliminated under Bercovici's plan. All those discussions that take place among the Japanese in private—which Blackthorne never heard and would not have understood anyway—would have to go if the script were done from Blackthorne's point of view. In the book, the Japanese talked among themselves in English. That would not work smoothly on the screen. The Japanese view of alien Westerners—bearded, scraggly, smelly, and bad-mannered—would have to be implicit in what was shown.

Opposite page:
Awaiting Hiromatsu's arrival.

Below:
Hiromatsu comes to Anjiro.

Clavell handed a thinned-out copy of the book back to Bercovici, with paragraphs crossed out and whole pages missing.

"All right. It works," he said. And that copy of *Shōgun* stayed on Bercovici's desk throughout the writing of the script.

There is no question that Bercovici's approach subtly changed *Shōgun's* basic perspective. Clavell himself notes that, in the novel, Blackthorne is the alien. "It's a Japanese story, a very pro-Japanese story." In the beginning, we are not at all sure that Blackthorne is a hero. His crude, sometimes scheming ways do not compare favorably to the clean, philosophical society he encounters. Only as he finds the beauty of Japan do we find the beauty in his character.

By switching the perspective from the Japanese to Black-

thorne, all is reversed. Blackthorne becomes a hero and it is Japan that is alien. When we first see him on the deck of the Erasmus in the film version, he is a quite recognizable Western hero. Says Clavell simply, "Different media. You don't relate film form to book form."

As one looks through the hefty script, there are long scenes of untranslated Japanese. The best the English reader can do is to skip over them. But all of those lines were translated into English for the use of the director, Jerry London, and his task was to make those scenes coherent to an audience that would not understand a word of what was being said. Bercovici had carefully chosen the Japanese scenes to be self-explanatory. The action, the expressions on the actors' faces, a gesture here, a prop there, would have to carry the meaning.

Blackthorne watches
as Rodrigues bluffs
his way aboard
the _Erasmus._

"The main consideration," says Bercovici, "was to write a script that takes place in Japan in 1600 and introduces an audience to Japan in the same way that the main character in the story is introduced to Japan. My noble ambition is that as Blackthorne learns Japanese—30 or 40 basic words of Japanese—the audience at the end of 12 hours of *Shōgun* will know more Japanese than they did at the beginning.

‡ ‡ ‡

By the spring of 1979, the principal elements of the production team had been assembled. Preliminary research into sets, costumes, and samurai lore was going on at the Paramount lot. Contractors and technicians were figuring out what equipment they would need to take along and what they might expect to find in Japan. Connections were being made with the Japanese participants on everything from use of studios to accomodations for the crew.

Blackthorne and company were ready to leave for Japan.

Shin Nishida and
some of his costume
designs.

KIKU

EITHER

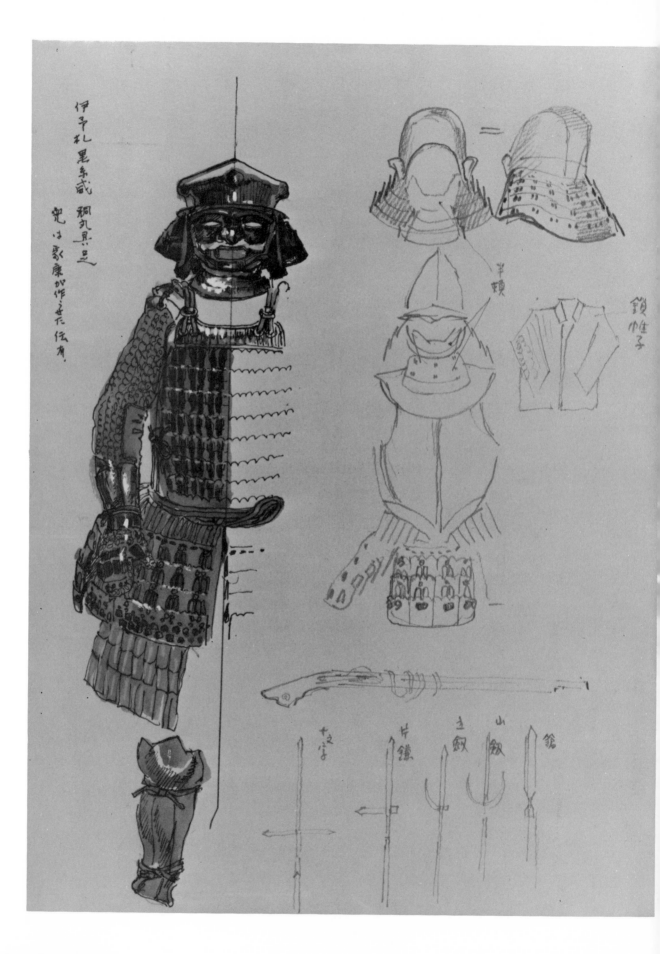

伊予札黒糸威
胴丸具足
兜は家康が作らせた伝有.

半頬

鎖帷子

十文字　片鎌　十手　山鉄　銛

Hiromatsu

陣羽織

佩楯（腰鎧）

侍大将

Samurai

A DAIMYO   FULL DRESS   FORMAL CLOTHES FOR DAIMYO

NAGA
(FUJIOKA HIROSHI)

OMI YUKI MEGURO

門番

SAMURAI GUARD AT
GATE

Bree ches
指貫
SASHINUKI

羽織姿 は GOWNS FOR SAMURAI

活作時外 国

女性髪型① (KIRI GYOKO ORYURIKO YABUS MOTHER

HAIR·STYLE FOR WOMEN

A.D.1573〜1688

A.D.1650

A.D. 1573〜1688

唐輪まげ からわ

兵庫まげ

唐輪

唐輪

下げ髪

玉結び

Getting Started

The filmmakers had an advantage over Blackthorne. They could prepare for their stay in Japan. They were not the first of their people to make it through the narrow straits to the East, plopped down in a new world. They had, at least in theory, a chance to preview what they might be getting themselves into.

Director Jerry London did that by looking at Japanese films, one a day for six weeks. He ran all the classic Japanese films, looked at filmmaker Akira Kurosawa's work for a second time, and reviewed samurai movies for their scenes of seppuku and Ninja warrior attacks. He wasn't studying their directing techniques as much as he was trying to prepare himself for what he might encounter in Japanese film studios. "It gave me a clue as to what actors or what type of scenes the Japanese might lean toward, and then I used it as a tool to work from. It also gave me a feel for the authenticity and the look of the period. I wanted to see what *they* did. So when I got there and I saw a Ninja warrior for the first time, it really *wasn't* the first time—I had already seen it on film."

A Ninja warrior.

He also mapped out the 600-page script scene-by-scene, so that if, as inevitably happens in such a long production, the shooting schedule were to be changed, he would be prepared to shift gears quickly into a different scene and not lose valuable time. If an actor got sick or a set wasn't ready or a location fell through, he might find himself having to shoot whatever else he could get sets and actors for. On the third day of shooting, he might need to jump to a scene originally planned for the 60th day. That called for knowing the script backwards and forwards.

Once in Japan, much of the research was left to the Japanese. Toho Studios provided a Japanese crew, three studios, miscellaneous equipment, and technical advisors. The principal contribution of the Japanese was to make sure everything was accurate. In Tokyo, Bercovici went over his script with a Japanese writer who had written a number of samurai films and was very familiar with the period. The Japanese writer pointed out a few historical inaccuracies and changed some of the names of minor characters to make them more authentic. At the same time, the American set designer and construction coordinator worked closely with the Japanese art director and set coordinator. "The research they did saved me the effort," says London. "They knew exactly what should be there to make it authentic. In fact, in most of the sets, the walls were hand-painted by [costume designer] Shin Nishida."

Left:
Jerry London — "a feel for the look of the period."

Bottom:
Shin Nishida handpainted sets and walls.

Other changes in the script were made when Bercovici started scouting locations at the beginning of May. Before he reached the Orient, he had been working on a great, limitless landscape that existed somewhere in his own mind. Once in Japan, he began to make the changes that were required by the realities of the situation. For instance, in one scene from the book, the pilot Rodrigues is swept overboard in the storm and washes up on the shore. Yabu and several samurai search along the coastline until they find him at the bottom of a steep cliff. A complicated rescue ensues in which Yabu climbs down to get Rodrigues while the tide is coming in. A samurai throws himself off the cliff, giving up his life in order to alert Yabu to the tide. It is one of the first dramatic demonstrations of samurai mores.

Opposite page:
Rodrigues overboard.

Below:
Storm at sea.

Bercovici took stock of the locations he was looking at and figured it would cost two weeks and "a lotta money" to do that scene. He had yet to find a suitable cliff, for one thing, which probably would mean a special trip to another island. Instead he took out his script and rewrote the scene, trying to cut the costs while still keeping the drama. The solution was to have Rodrigues rescued as soon as he is swept overboard. Blackthorne, with standard heroics, jumps in right after Rodrigues and starts swimming towards him. Yabu, not to be outdone, throws himself into the ocean right behind Blackthorne, and together they drag Rodrigues back on deck.

Throughout the production, the Americans were very careful to keep things authentic. "The Japanese were very nervous that we were going to make a picture they would laugh at in Japan," says Bercovici. "We did not want to make that kind of picture. We wanted to be legitimate about it."

Like Bercovici, London had been involved in other long-form television projects, such as Arthur Hailey's *Wheels* and Irwin Shaw's *Evening in Byzantium*. But shooting on location added a whole new twist to *Shōgun*. "My philosophy as a director is to let each scene tell me what to do," says London. "I don't have a style as such, except that I knew that when I was shooting a picture with this kind of scope, I wanted to see everything. I knew I would be using wider lenses than I normally shoot with because we were picking good locations that worked for that period. Usually when you do period pieces you have to limit yourself in your shooting because there are so many things you *shouldn't* see. In Japan, I wasn't trying to hide *anything*. You'll see many shots that show vistas of 360 degrees. We could sweep a whole valley or show the water of Anjiro and the hills. I think the beauty that we captured will do a lot for tourism in Japan. It was a marvelous opportunity to open up."

On the indoor scenes, London and cinematographer Andy Laszlo worked to develop a good formula for the lighting and photography. The goal was a "soft, pastelly look of woodblock prints," explains London. "For the love scenes, we did a lot of low-key, back-lit, artistic lighting. Any scene where Blackthorne and Mariko are together, there's a different mood to the lighting."

Jerry London and Andy Laszlo.

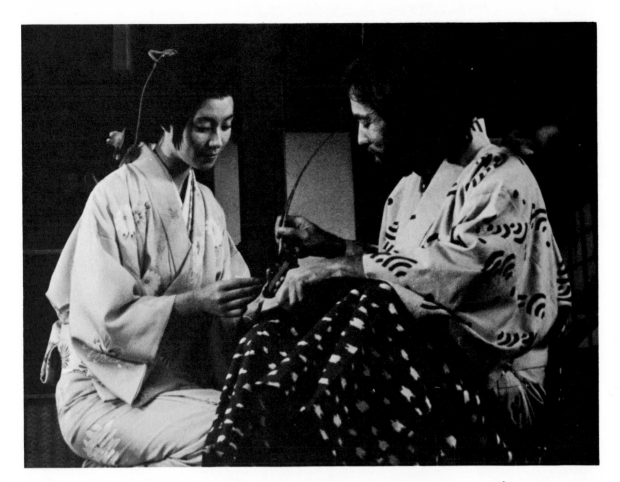

Shōgun presented London with virtually every kind of technical and logistical problem that can be encountered in a film, from comedy scenes to battle scenes to love scenes, from ship scenes to traveling shots, from low-key lighting to high-key lighting. Every lens and filter in the camera bag was hauled out at one time or another—split diopters, neutral density filters, all the zoom lenses.

Editing was an additional consideration. There were two editing teams, one in Japan and one at home, and two sets of dailies. One set stayed in Japan and was edited for the 12-hour television version. The set that went home was shown to Paramount and NBC and edited for the two-and-a-half-hour theatrical version.

Within a short time, London was beginning to feel like Blackthorne himself. "Here I am in this strange country, trying to do this impossible task, and Blackthorne, too, is a man who came to a strange country and tried to survive and was really unsure whether he was leaving or wasn't leaving."

Low-key lighting for Richard's scenes with Yoku.

Below:
First Assistant —
Director Charlie Bjarko.

Bottom:
Frank Cardea,
Production Executive.

To play the part of Blackthorne, London was looking for someone who could take a "straight line approach" to the character—"just let it happen and be innocent enough to understand what's happening to him." He found his man in Richard Chamberlain.

Chamberlain, who had moved from the stereotyped television character of *Doctor Kildare* to a variety of distinguished roles ranging from Hamlet to Wild Bill Hickok, had been after the part of Blackthorne for some time. After reading *Shōgun*, he was so enthused that, long before the film became a possibility, he organized a trip to Japan for himself just to see what all the excitement was about. He saw the character as "very shrewd, very strong, intensely ambitious. The idea that *he* made it to Japan first meant an enormous amount to him, I think. It was like conquering Everest. He sought fame and he sought fortune, with great skill and determination. On the other hand, he had a very sensitive side. His dealings with Mariko were very sensitive and loving. I think she opened up a whole area of his being he didn't even know about. And he dealt with Toranaga and all those guys very shrewdly, although he was certainly extremely manipulated by them. I don't think he liked his crew much. As time went on, he began to detest them."

What was Chamberlain's approach? "Damned if *I* know. I just mainly tried to find his growth, his civilization. He was a rough, filthy European when he arrived and was gradually civilized by these 'heathens.' His sensitivities were enlivened by his love affair with Mariko. And I tried to find that growth and hang onto it because, of course, we didn't shoot in sequence. I tried to see it all through his eyes, all this new and amazingly different culture. But *I* don't know how I find a character. It's definitely not an intellectual process with me. It's more a matter of feeling into it, going over it, reading the novel, reading the script, trying to find the dynamics."

Chamberlain is generally congratulated for not only bringing a warm, friendly air to the set but, by his complete professionalism, enabling the complicated project to be finished on schedule. "With another actor in that role, the picture might never have been finished," says Bercovici wryly. "If we had had a troublemaker in the role of Blackthorne, and be-

lieve it or not there *are* actors who are troublemakers, he could have killed us. Halfway into the picture, when you can't replace 'em, they do it to you and you're dead. They do two takes and say, 'Whatever you got, you got, and I ain't gonna do any more!' Never once did Richard. No actor ever worked harder."

There's a scene on the steps of Osaka castle when Blackthorne goes into a mad dance in order to divert attention and allow his companions to escape a group of unfriendly samurai. The hike up those steps was such that most of the crew went up once in the morning and thought twice about coming down for lunch. Chamberlain, on the other hand, was being asked to run up and down all day long.

"Jerry, he's gonna die," said Bercovici to London at one point. "You can't do any more."

"One more, just one more," said London.

"OK, but the second Richard complains, I'm pulling the plug and you've got what you've got."

Up and down, up and down, Blackthorne's mad dance continued, until he came walking towards the director, panting heavily. Bercovici was ready to call a halt.

"Listen," puffed Chamberlain. "Just give me five minutes, can you? And I'll do it again."

Chamberlain credits his experience in television with teaching him the pleasures of hard work. "I had a lot riding on this. And I like to work hard anyway. I think that's one thing I learned from *Doctor Kildare*. It was incredibly hard work, and I sort of got used to it. A lot of actors start out being pampered in films and they don't know what hard work is. But I don't think of it as anything special.

"Television is such a technical medium, speed is so necessary, and the technical side takes so much time, that by the time it gets around to do the scene with the actors, it's 'OK, come on, let's get this done. Damn it, you did it wrong! Let's do it again. Shit!'

"The actors are just supposed to *do* it, man. And you don't get any rehearsal and you don't get any sort of care. The actor in television is very much on his own."

Right:
Naga, Blackthorne,
and Rodrigues.

Below:
Yabu and Hiromatsu
arrive at Osaka.

Opposite page:
Naga orders
Blackthorne to
remain on the galley.

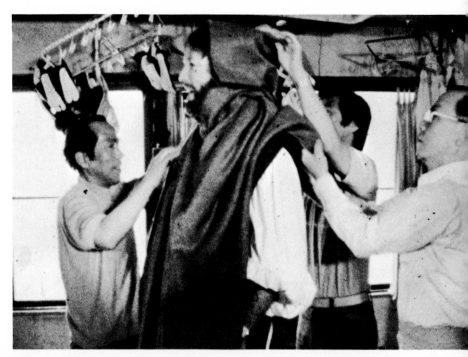

Warm, friendly, and a complete professional.

London cast the rest of the English-speaking roles from the English stage. The Japanese originally recommended that Japanese actors with a command of English play the parts of the Jesuit priests, but London felt that would have been confusing. The Jesuits were, after all, Occidentals who had learned Japanese. It would be better if they spoke native English and learned Japanese, phonetically if need be.

It's easy to lump the English-speaking cast into "Blackthorne's crew" or "the Jesuits." But London saw individual characters among the crew and priests, and went after actors who could bring out that individuality:

"Alan Badel, who plays dell'Aqua, is a very intriguing actor who gives you anything but the norm. He's very unpredictable and makes himself very interesting on film.

Alan Badel as
Father dell'Aqua.

"Damien Thomas, who plays Alvito, is a terrific stage actor and adapted well to film.

"John Rhys-Davies, who plays Rodrigues, has a terrific sense of humor, which is what I was looking for in the part. He's bigger than life but he's real.

"Ed Peel, who plays Pieterzoon, has very small moments in the picture, but they are alive and dynamic.

"George Innes, who plays Vinck, has a fantastic scene in Part Five where he goes mad.

"Every one of these men has a moment in the film. The seven or eight men who play the crew of the <u>Erasmus</u> each have their own distinct personalities. We know them for a short time, but we see the individuality of each one. That's what we went for."

Above:
John Rhys-Davies —
"bigger than life
but real."

Left:
George Innes as
Vinck.

Right:
Steve Ubels a Roper.

Below:
Leon Lissek as
Father Sebastio.

Bottom:
Wladek Sheybal as
Ferriera.

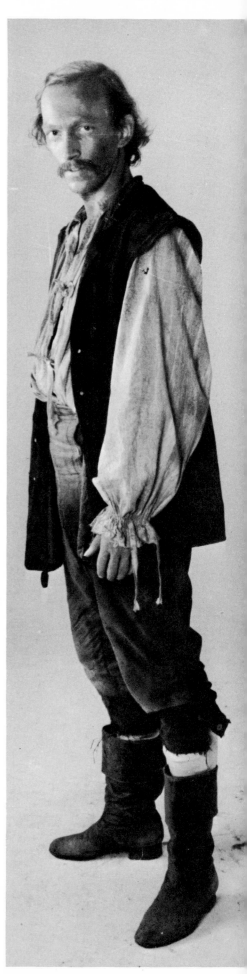

Left: Eric Richard as Maetsukker.
Below and bottom: Neil McCarthy as Spillbergen.

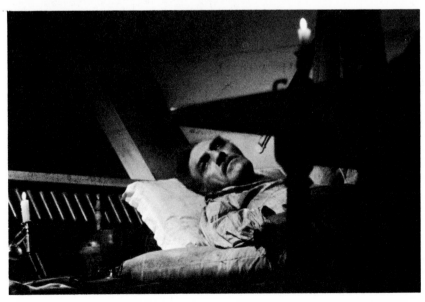

Right: Stewart
MacKenzie as Croocq.
Below: Ian Jentle
as Salamon.
Below center: Morgan
Sheppard as Specz.
Bottom: John Carney
as Ginsel.

The role of Toranaga, the future Shōgun, went to Japan's premier international actor, Toshiro Mifune.

"I think Mifune *is* Toranaga," says London. "He's a man of great dignity. He was the most prepared actor of all. He was always the first one on the set, made up, ready to go. And he understood the part. He was very helpful in the staging of the extras and enthusing them. The extras were a bunch of college kids and he'd get out there and make a speech and get 'em all pumped up."

"I think Mifune *is* Toshiro Mifune," says Bercovici. "There are some things he will do. There are some things he will *not* do."

Bercovici does concede, though, that Mifune got into the role of Toranaga right from the start and never got out of it. He once invited the American crew for "a little informal cocktail party, come as you are," and when they arrived in their jeans and Windbreakers, he was standing there in a white tuxedo over a catered spread of ice statues and boats made out of salmon. On the last day of filming, in an out-of-the-way, distinctly non-elegant studio, he managed to throw a party for the crew complete with servants in white jackets and gloves.

But while Bercovici felt that Mifune was into a game of one-upmanship, Chamberlain saw it as method acting. "He's quite sweet when he's in his civvies. But the minute he puts his costume on, he is a samurai. He just sits in a corner and growls. And he looks *incredibly* forbidding. You wouldn't *dare* go up and talk to him. But he did some of the most astonishing things."

In one scene, after an army of samurai had ridden through, there was an ominous sound of hoofbeats in the distance. Mifune came charging in on a large and skittish horse, headed right for the center of the scene. The other actors thought they were going to be crushed by an out-of-control horse, when Mifune suddenly stopped, dismounted effortlessly from his horse and went on with the scene.

This impressive demonstration of horse-handling was repeated for the cameras nine times. On the last take, the horse veered to the left to avoid having his sore mouth reined in again, and Mifune took a rather serious tumble. His only reaction was to apologize profusely for having been injured.

Above:
An audience with
Toranaga.

Left:
Blackthorne is
taken to prison.

Opposite page:
Osaka Castle.

The Making of *Shōgun*   83

TORANAGA

Kosode

aishi

Dofuku

Sashinuki

Tabi

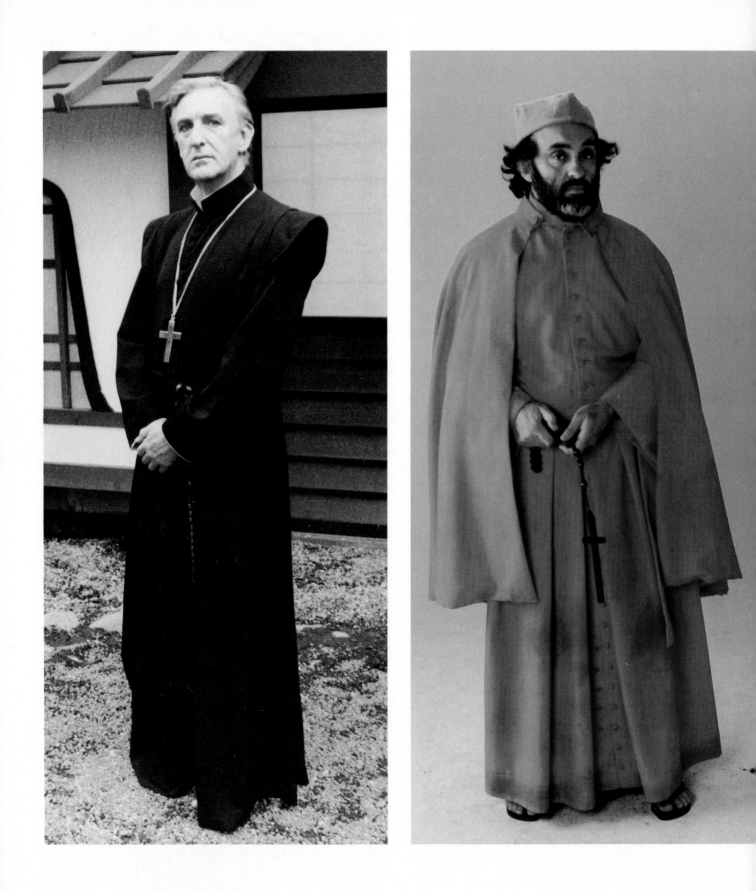

The hardest part to cast was Mariko, since the story called for a Japanese actress who spoke fluent English and could act in both languages. At one point, author Clavell, appearing on a Japanese television show, mentioned that he was still looking for a Mariko and invited members of the audience to submit applications. But the part ultimately went to an actress well-known in Japan, Yoko Shimada.

Shimada's introduction to American audiences was hampered slightly by her troubles with English pronunciation. But constant coaching from Luca Bercovici, dialogue coach and son of the producer, helped her over that. And there was little problem establishing rapport with her co-star. "She was the perfect vision of traditional Japanese femininity," says Chamberlain. "Watching her open a shoji screen is almost an orgasmic experience."

Richard Chamberlain and Yoko Shimada.

Rapport was no problem.

"The perfect vision."

With Yaemon and
Lady Kiri nearby,
Toranaga asks
about Blackthorne's
origins. Mariko
is the interpreter.

Casting the rest of the large Japanese cast—over 100 parts—presented problems. The Americans were looking at over 60 videotapes a day, tests of actors who were completely unknown to them, speaking in a language they could not understand, and they had $22 million riding on their choices. "We had to tread a very careful line," says Bercovici. "We, the American audience, may not have understood what the Japanese were saying, but *they* sure as hell understood what they were saying." One stunning actress had Bercovici and London won over, when a Japanese assistant said, "We cannot use her. She *cannot* speak. She's awful." With regret, they heeded the words.

Japanese actors, for the most part, have a different style of acting than American actors. Kabuki acting is still favored—big stage gestures, big emotion, projection—what we would call overacting. Japanese stunts are choreographed so beautifully that they look like ballet.

Left:
Frankie Sakai as Yabu.

Right:
Toru Abe as Hiromatsu.

Top: Hideo Takamatsu as Buntaro.
Above: Mika Kitagawa as Kiku.
Right: Yosuke Natsuki as Zataki.

Far left:
Shin Takuma as
Naga.

Left:
Seiji Miyaguchi
as Muraji.

Below left:
Rinichi Yamamoto
as Yoshinaka.

Below:
Yuki Meguro as Omi.

But for an American audience, London wanted realism. He needed spontaneous action scenes, not rhythmic sword play and graceful dying gestures. And he got that by taking the basic Japanese style and paring away the excess. "The best thing you can do for a director is to give him too much," he says. "Let him take away. It's when you have to start adding and they can't do it that you get in trouble. I would explain to them that when a guy gets stabbed and dies, he dies *then*. He doesn't do a flop-over with his arms in the air, and go 'Ohhhhhh!' and make big sweeping gestures. They'd do a scene and I'd say, 'That's good. Now take *this* out, take *this* out. Don't do this. Don't do *this*.' Once you got the first scene in the can the way you wanted it, they understood what we were after. From then on it was easy. They were terrific."

And despite the fact that it would often take 15 minutes to communicate a stage direction to a Japanese actor through an interpreter, London claims he had no problem working with actors who did not speak his language. "An actor is an actor. And it's all in their eyes and their attitude. You either believe them or you don't. When we videotaped the tests, even though I didn't speak any Japanese, I could tell whether I believed them or not."

In the film there are scenes that go for seven or eight minutes without a break—entirely in Japanese. The script was constructed so that these could be made intelligible to the American audience via context, gestures, and facial expressions. If the audience did *not* understand what was going on, that was on purpose too, to add mystery and intrigue. Attitudes, shifts, positions, props, anything that could be used to convey a meaning without words came into play. For instance, when the Japanese were talking about a pistol, they would gesture to it. They would point to people they were talking about and raise their voices if they were supposed to be upset.

In a typical scene, Mariko's husband Buntaro is telling Toranaga that he knows about Blackthorne and Mariko. He thinks that Blackthorne should be eliminated. Occasionally the word *Anjin* pops up, which we know is Blackthorne's Japanese name, a word which means pilot. Toranaga looks upset and casts a glance at Mariko, and we grasp that he knows about her

Left:
Frankie Sakai and
Toshiro Mifune.

Below:
Communicating a
simple direction.

*Without a word
of English.*

liason with Blackthorne. Then he says something to Buntaro in a stern voice, and we can imagine that he is saying something like, "Don't ever speak to me of this again!"

Later, Buntaro confronts Mariko alone. He is obviously upset and takes out his sword. He is yelling at her and she is yelling at him, and he raises his sword above his head. She bows her head and says something in Japanese—"Kill me," perhaps. It is a dramatic scene between the two actors, conveying information and emotion, all without a word of English.

‡ ‡ ‡

If the Japanese had additional thoughts about the making of *Shōgun* at this point, they kept them to themselves. Although it was a film about Japan, made in Japan, with Japanese actors and Japanese facilities, and addressing itself to a period of Japanese history very familiar to any Japanese citizen, it was in the end an American film. Ninety-eight percent of the Japanese historical corrections were accepted. But on at least one occasion, artistic concerns outvoted historical accuracy.

In a park at Hikone, Japanese assistants started scaring a group of swans away just before shooting started.

"What are they doing?" shouted London. "I want the swans in the scene. It's great. I love it."

And Bercovici ordered, "Bring the swans back."

"No, no," said the assistant. "You see, swans didn't come to Japan until 40 years later."

As it turned out, there *were* swans in Japan in 1600, but the Japanese had not yet learned how to clip their wings and make them stay. At any rate, it was decided that 40 years' difference between fact and fiction was not that big a deal, and the swans stayed.

"I did not make friends by doing that," Bercovici concedes. "I suppose it's as if the Japanese came to America to make a picture about the American Civil War and had Indians fighting on the side of the South. The Americans might say, 'No, no, that's not right.' And the Japanese might answer, 'Yes, but it's really *very* good!'"

Filming in Tokyo began June 4, 1979, at the Toho Studios. The filmmakers originally hoped to shoot some scenes inside historical temples and castles. But the risk was too great. The doors, hand-painted, 900-year-old sliding shoji screens, were national treasures. It would have been necessary to remove them and store them—*carefully*—and replace them with copies. All the tatami floor mats would have had to be replaced as well. And despite all precautions, it would have been hard to avoid tracking mud in from outside as generators, lights, cables, and cameras were moved here and there. If, at some point, the Japanese had changed their minds, or been offended by some damage to their sacred shrines, the crew would have been left with no sets and a big hole in the shooting schedule.

Somehow the familiar confines of a film studio seemed much safer. But even the studio required making some adjustments. To retain authenticity meant painting 100 faithful copies of the priceless shojis and spending up to $5,000 apiece on silk kimonos. And the Japanese studios simply did not offer the facilities American film crews normally expect. The Japanese do not bother soundproofing their studios, since they usually add the sound later. Many of their floors are dirt, which makes them more adaptable to Japanese needs. They do not use

Chapman cranes or camera cars. And their lighting equipment, by American standards, is heavy and cumbersome.

Camera operator Chuy Elizondo quickly discovered that he was not in America. First, he found that things were not organized the same way. In the way he was used to working, the director of photography discusses the photography with the director and then, with the help of a gaffer, takes care of the lighting. The camera operator takes care of anything that has to do with moving the camera, and he has an assistant who focuses, zooms, and takes care of the equipment.

In Japan, he found, the director of photography also operates the camera. But he does not touch the lighting. He has one assistant who does nothing but focus, another who operates nothing but the zoom, and a third who does nothing but take light readings.

The lighting was a bit behind the times, by Elizondo's standards. "They use cold lights, kind of like still photographers use. You can probably buy them for $2.50 at Thrifty. And they use rice paper in front of them. And they have just a simple clamp on it. When they put the light on, if you don't watch it carefully, the clamp slides and the lighting changes. The overall feeling of the light is much different from what *we* use.

"We use bigger lights, all on stands. If you want to diffuse the light, you have certain things already set up and you can just tell an electrician 'put a single' or 'put a double.'"

For lighting and camera work, it turned out that using Japanese technicians created too much of a communication problem. Rather than do battle with different customs and a different language, the Americans sent home for Elizondo plus an American gaffer, best-boy, and electrician.

In other areas, though, the American crew was committed to forging ahead with Japanese assistants. All Bob Dawson wanted for his special effects crew were a few good carpenters he could count on from beginning to end. The Japanese misunderstood at first and started sending him high school kids parttime. When he finally did get his message across, he found that there were no general handymen in Japan. Everyone specialized. "There might be a man who specializes in smoke, and that's all he does for a living—he comes into the studio and he does smoke. And then another guy will do fire, and all he does is fire. The four men I had weren't even carpenters."

He wanted the kind of special effects assistants he was used to at home, the kind who could help him build a platform or a safety barricade at a moment's notice. But he was told by the studio manager, "We don't have personnel like that. We don't have effects men."

"Just give me four willing bodies, then," he asked.

Even with four willing bodies, he found himself constantly looking over their shoulders, making sure they understood what he wanted. Often he just gave up and did it himself.

Quality, dedication, and authenticity.

The great care and pride that the Japanese take in their work was, in this case, not what the Americans really needed. They were more concerned with meeting a deadline. The Japanese set painters were outstanding. But they did not use spray guns, and when stand-by sets were needed on a day's notice, they did not know how to respond. American set carpenters make false floors out of cheap wood with a thin veneer of good wood, but the Japanese build *quality* floors, no matter what the purpose. From the American point of view, such quality and dedication were not really necessary on the screen as no one would see them.

Dawson thought he had cleverly prepared his construction drawings by measuring them all in the metric system. Then it turned out that the older Japanese carpenters use their own measuring system, called shaku. (A tenth of a shaku measure equals just about a foot, English measure.) So he went out and bought a couple of Japanese rulers and re-drew everything in shaku.

He also found that, when buildings are constructed, rooms are measured by the number of tatami mats they will hold: The Japanese build four-tatami rooms, six-tatami rooms, etc. But the tatamis in Tokyo are a different size than the tatamis in Kyoto. More confusion!

In Japan, one does not walk on the tatamis with shoes on. They cost about $250 for a 2 × 5 foot mat, for one thing, and they are delicate. But it is more than that. "It's not just a custom," says Elizondo. "It's almost a religion." The studio sets were covered with tatamis, which the Americans had paid for and which were solely for use in filming. But the Japanese were adamant about the no-shoes rule. One scene involved burning a set that was covered with tatami mats. The Japanese objected to walking on even the burnt tatamis.

For the Americans, it was fun at first—taking their shoes off to go onto the set. But after several months, winter arrived. The Japanese stages were not heated, and 35 to 40 degrees is not barefoot weather in America. By that time, taking off shoes, putting them on, and taking them off again every time they had to go outside for a piece of equipment—and that was often—was becoming downright annoying.

Some Americans began to wear heavy shoes and deliberately walk around on the mats, which did succeed in offending the Japanese. Others were more open to the Japanese culture. "Some of their methods are much different from ours and the only thing to do is to adapt to theirs," said construction coordinator Al DeGaetano. "Otherwise, you'd be beating your brains out."

Molding rocks at Toho studios.

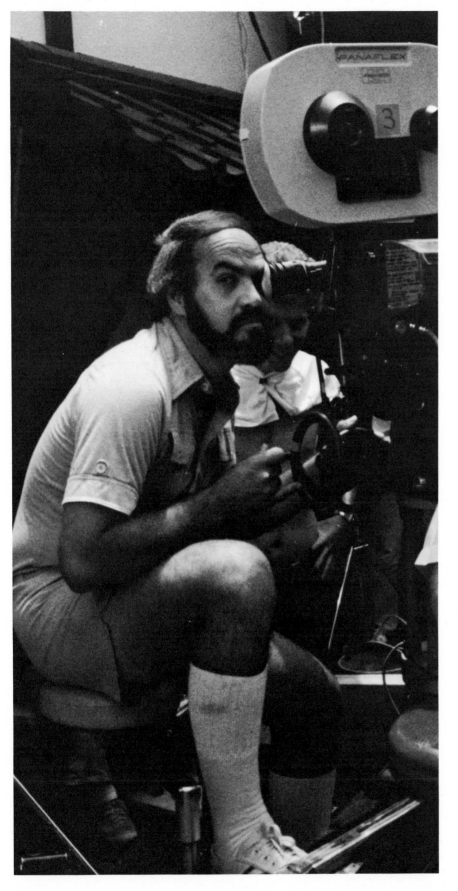

Chuy Elizondo
checks a scene.

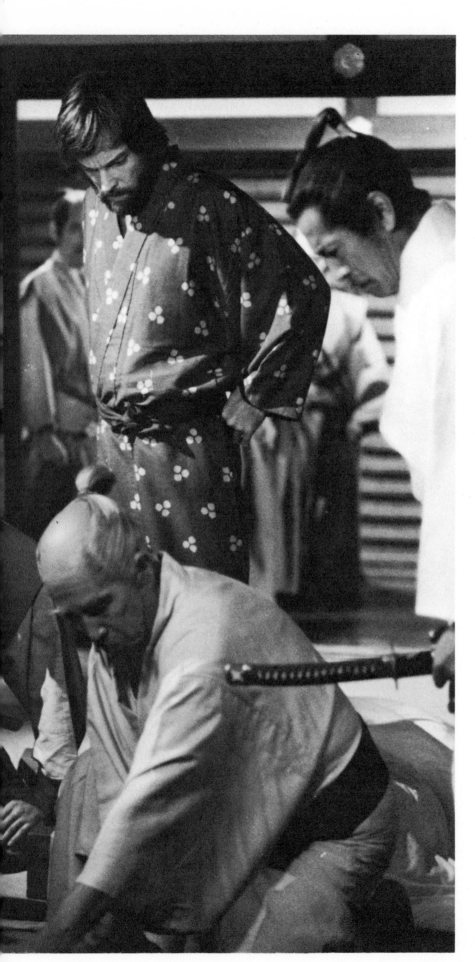

Opposite page:
Blackthorne is
attacked in Osaka
Castle.

Left:
Hiromatsu
discovers a tattoo —
the would-be
assassin is an
Amida Tong.

Below:
Tea with Kako,
Sono, and Asa.

Opposite page:
Toranaga, Mariko,
and Blackthorne
escape Osaka Castle.

This page:
The mad dance up
and down the castle
steps — "Just give me
five minutes and
I'll do it again."

Right:
Roast capon, fresh
bread, and wine —
Blackthorne stuffs
himself.

Below and opposite
page: Ferriera offers
Toranaga and
Mariko shelter on
the Black Ship — in
return for
Blackthorne.

Japanese work crews, for instance, did not have a foreman who could carry out the orders from the top. "They work in groups and they *discuss* everything," notes DeGaetano philosophically. "Here, you go to the foreman and you tell him what you want. Over there, they don't work that way. One fella comes in and he may decide to work on the ceiling. Somehow it all works out in the end."

Japanese actors, it turned out, worked only by the day. It was impossible to hire them for the length of the production, as is usually the case at home. It was actually necessary to sit down with each actor's representative and look at the schedule to find out when they would be available. Some scenes were held up because an actor had already signed up for work that day on another project. Even Mifune was making another film simultaneously, in Korea. Bercovici would find himself on the phone bargaining with the other producer over a long distance connection: "Look, you can have him Thursday if we can have him Wednesday and you put him on a plane and fly him in."

Toranaga inspects Yabu's troops at Anjiro.

"We were going nuts," says Bercovici. "They were all working on different projects—two days here, one day here. And there must be a lotta work in Japan, because they're always working. It was impossible for us to schedule accurately even two months in advance."

Add to that the problem of doing all this through interpreters, and one begins to suspect it was not exactly smooth going in Japan. Bob Dawson found that even inviting one of his assistants to have a cup of coffee and a donut took seven or eight minutes. He has no idea what they were talking about, but he imagines it was a simple argument:

"He wants you to have a cup of coffee and a donut with him."

"What's a donut?"

"It's an American sweet roll with a hole in it."

"Oh. Well, that's OK, but I don't like coffee."

"He just wants you to sit down and eat something with him."

"What does he want to talk about?"

"I don't know."

"Well . . . tell him I'll just have a glass of milk."

On the job, it became even more complicated.

"I need this wall built and this piece of steel cut right away," Dawson might tell the interpreter. And then the interpreter and the assistant would start talking away in Japanese.

"What's all the conversation about?" Dawson would ask. "I just need a simple job done."

"Well," answers the interpreter, "he's wondering why you want it cut here and why you want it welded here. Why don't we do it *this* way and bolt it?"

"That isn't what I want. I need you to do exactly what I tell you. Interpret that."

"Well, I am, Bob, but he's wondering about . . ."

"Never mind," says Dawson. "I'll do it myself."

Part of his problem was that he was trying to communicate technical ideas through interpreters who were not familiar with his trade. The interpreter's English might be excellent, but if she did not know the difference between a knee brace and an I-beam, she certainly couldn't tell the Japanese assistant about it. So Dawson would hear Japanese sentences that contained words like "knee brace" and "I-beam"—in English, not Japanese. At that point he got an inkling of why his assistant was looking at him as if he were some kind of mental deficient. His message was not getting across.

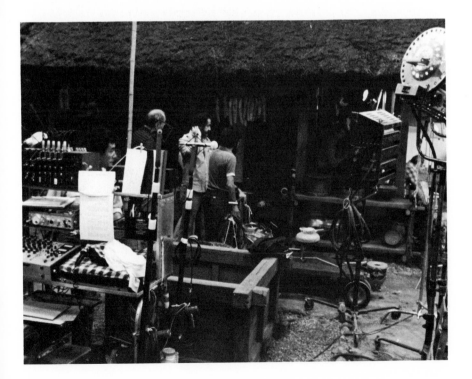

Right:
A new house in Anjiro—and a new consort, Fujiko.

Below:
Fujiko guards Blackthorne's pistol while he goes with Omi to see Lord Yabu.

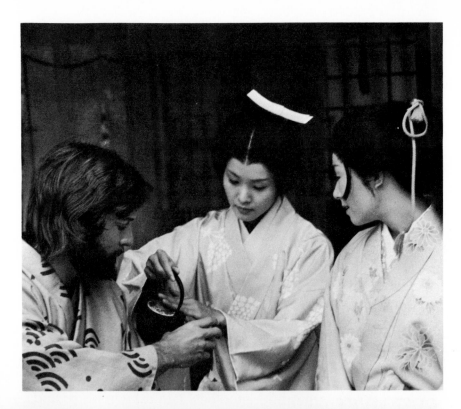

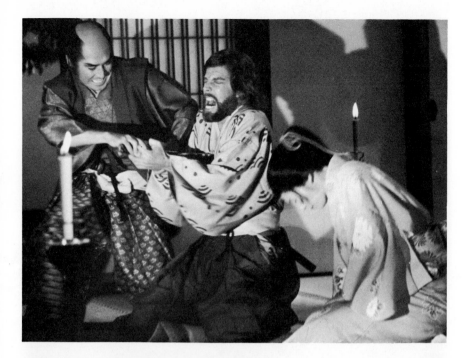

*Top:
Blackthorne attempts
seppuku.*

*Left:
Blackthorne with
Fujiko.*

Even the Japanese version of the script somehow got changed in the translation. Bercovici and London would be launching into a scene, look up, and note that the Japanese actors were doing and saying the exact opposite of what was in the script. Someone would bring the Japanese version over and translate it and, sure enough, the Japanese were following their directions to the letter—except that they were the wrong directions.

Above:
Mariko, badly beaten
by Buntaro, is
confronted by
Blackthorne.

Opposite page
Fujiko asks
Blackthorne to
kill her.

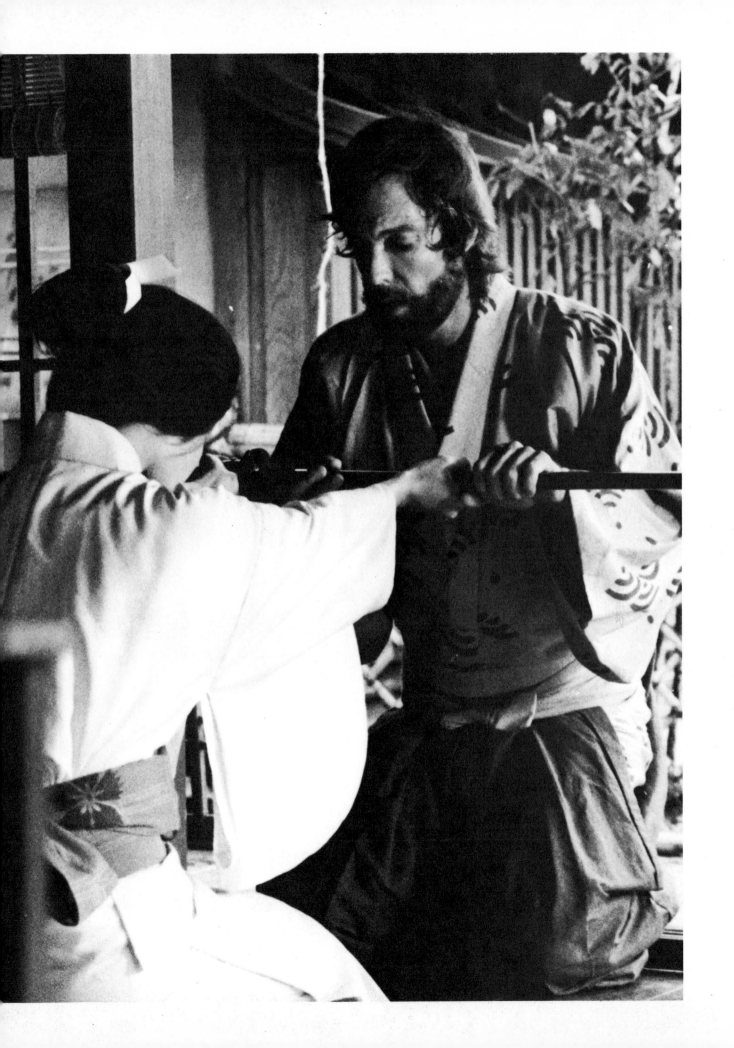

And, of course, speaking through interpreters every time there was something to be said made it rather difficult to establish warm personal relationships. "I didn't get to know many of those guys well," says Dawson. "I didn't feel any resentment as far as they were concerned. It was just that we did not know how to communicate. And their way of doing things was different. They don't use power tools like skill saws. So these guys would be hacking away at a piece of timber with their hand saws and I would come over with my chain saw and they just loved it. But they'd go right back to their old way of doing it. They were scared of it, for one thing, and in that respect it was probably better, because if you're scared of it you probably end up cutting your leg off."

The Japanese way of work evidently did not include frantic dashes to meet last-minute deadlines. And they probably led much calmer lives as a result. But those Americans who were tied to a tight schedule did not know quite how to communicate their haste. They tried the old trick of saying that the work was due tomorrow when it really wasn't due until next week, but even then they learned to feel nervous when the Japanese said, "Don't worry about it. We'll have it ready."

Often it was not ready. But, as Dawson says, "You don't change spots on a leopard. You just sit back and grit your teeth and hope to God it will rub off on them that we are excited and we want to see what the finished product will look like. They were more than willing, from the grips on down to the electricians and the carpenters, and they did their best. They were fighting two elements there—their way of doing things and our way of doing things. I have no bad feelings about them at all. They are a wonderful people."

‡ ‡ ‡

The storm sequences at sea were filmed in a large water tank at Toho Studios. But the tank was like nothing Toho—or the neighbors who lived near Toho—had ever seen before.

The Japanese did most of their special effects in miniature. The American style of filmmaking called for building them full-scale. It took 28 days to fill the tank with water. The water ran only at night, because when the tanks were filling, most of the surrounding neighborhood was without water. In

Below and opposite page: Building the samurai village.

the tank was a "gimbal"—and if you don't know what that is, just think how the Japanese felt. After Dawson despaired of interpreters and built them a working model of it, they understood: A gimbal was a floating platform, 12 × 50 feet, mounted on two axles so that it could turn like a boat in the water. Onto this gimbal were to be mounted full-size mock-ups of the <u>Erasmus</u> deck and the Japanese galley deck.

At first the gimbal was to be built just like they build 'em at home—with a hydraulic system. But in all of Japan there was

Filming a storm sequence in the Toho tank.

not a pump big enough to operate it. So the Americans switched to an air hoist with three-quarter-inch cable, shipped over from Paramount. Dawson had finally succeeded in communicating what a gimbal was. Now he had to explain that the ship mock-ups that were to fit over the gimbal had to be empty in the middle—and not solid, like a good, conscientious Japanese craftsman builds them.

That taken care of, all that was left was to hook up the air compressor. Dawson figured he would need, oh, about 100 pounds pressure. It never occurred to him that he would have any problem finding an air compressor of that capacity. But the standard in Japan was 45 to 50 pounds. In all of Japan, there were only two air compressors that could provide 100 pounds, and one of them was busy. By luck, one of the interpreters knew someone who knew how to lay hands on the other one, and the gimbal went into business.

After the first few days of shooting in Tokyo—the scene in which Blackthorne first wakes up in Japan—the crew moved over to the tanks. As you see the scene on the screen, Blackthorne is on the deck of the Erasmus at sea, being pelted with rain and shouting to his crew. Thunder and lightning cover the skies. If the camera were to draw back from the scene, you would see in the background large hoses spraying water into the air, banks of lights going on and off to provide lightning, a cutout of the Erasmus deck being rocked on a gimbal, and four large, incredibly noisy wind machines the size of jet engines.

The Japanese would have shot a scene like that during the day, using filters to make it look like night on film. But the American technique called for shooting night scenes at night. And at night, when the whole neighborhood was asleep, even the sound of a gaffer's voice traveled for blocks.

In Japan, there's a philosophical concept known as "ancient light." It's explained like this: If I own a house that has beautiful sunlight falling on it, and you come to build a taller house next to mine that cuts off the light, I have legal recourse and can prevent you from building. In the modern age of grassroots movements and individual rights, the idea of "ancient light" has new and original ramifications.

In this case, it applied to wind machines and water hoses. In Japan, a complaint by even one or two neighbors is taken seriously. A big buffer wall was built around the set and insulated walls were built around the wind machines. It cut down on the noise considerably—now it sounded like only a *minor* hurricane.

When, nevertheless, the *Shōgun* crew was informed that it would not be allowed to shoot after 10 at night, the diplomatic initiatives began. If it was getting dark at 7, by 10 they would be barely warmed up. Some kind of compromise was clearly needed. James Clavell wrote a letter to every home in the neighborhood, promising them autographed copies of *Shōgun* as soon as it appeared in Japanese. Producer Bercovici wrote a letter to every home, explaining what he was doing and inviting them all to come over to the studio and watch. Toshiro Mifune, an idol to movie-going Japanese, wrote a letter to every home, promising that there would be coffee and snacks at the studio for everyone.

The crew then proceeded to shoot through the night for several weeks. If anyone called the police, we will never know. For President Carter, it seems, was in Tokyo at that time for a summit meeting. While he was there, all available policemen were assigned to his security. If anyone registered a complaint about the tank, there was no one to check it out.

Neighborhood relations were finally patched up by delivery to every door of either a large bottle of sake or a coupon good for free beer, depending on who tells the story.

‡ ‡ ‡

The first month of shooting in Tokyo ended July 11. It was a month of reorganization and regrouping, of adapting to new surroundings, of trying to stay on schedule. But, most of all, it was a revealing introduction to Japan matched only by Blackthorne's.

One of the sets was a samurai street back lot at Ikuta, about 45 minutes from Toho. There was a crew of hundreds out there, and they were all entitled to one meal a day. Arrangements had been made to provide that meal from a catering truck, the only mobile kitchen in Japan.

One day it started to rain at Ikuta, so it was decided to
return to Toho and finish the day's shooting on an indoor stage
there. At the studio, Bercovici told a Japanese assistant to bring
the catering truck over from Ikuta for lunch.

"Sorry, we can't do that," he was told.

"Why not?"

"Because it's at Ikuta."

"I *know* it's at Ikuta. *Move* it. Move it from Ikuta to Toho."

"Oh, you can't move it."

"It's a mobile kitchen, isn't it?"

"Oh, yes! The only mobile kitchen in Japan!"

"Terrific! Mobilize it and mobilize it here."

"Uh, Uh. Can't do that."

"Why not?"

"Well, they didn't know that they had to move. If they had been told yesterday that they had to come here, then they could have come here. But it's too late to tell them now."

"Why?"

"They're not prepared for it."

Bercovici took a deep breath. "Look. Call them. Tell them to move the mobile kitchen from there to here so we can eat lunch."

"Can't do it."

This went on for ten minutes. Then Bercovici said, "Explain to me why the mobile kitchen, which *we're* renting, the only mobile kitchen in Japan, which has lunch there for all these people at Ikuta, why you can't bring the mobile kitchen from Ikuta to Toho."

The answer: "This is Japan."

At that, he gave up and everybody had sandwiches.

While Bob Dawson was wrestling with his gimbal, he also had a few special effects to figure out. Nothing fancy—just a few arrow-in-the-chest scenes, a nice fire for Mariko's cremation, and an earthquake. It was fairly standard stuff as far as Western filmmaking went. But this was Japan.

Arrows in the chest should have been a point where East and West could converge. After all, movie samurai have been getting arrows in the chest for almost as long as the U.S. Cavalry. But the samurai do it a little differently. Their arrows are the pop-up kind. The victim-to-be attaches a hidden arrow to his chest and, at the proper moment, hits the button that makes it pop up, so he can go into his dying routine. Or he may have his back to the camera when he is hit, only to whirl around in shock and display the arrow that has already been attached to him.

American arrows go in for a little more technology. The victim always takes his arrow on camera, so we can see every bloody detail. He wears a steel plate on his chest, to which is attached a piece of pine and a length of piano wire. The piano wire runs off camera to a special effects assistant, who is in charge of firing a hollow arrow that will run along the piano wire and impale itself at the receiving end—right smack on the piece of pine.

It came time for one of the English actors to get not one but three arrows in the chest. Dawson set up his three lengths of piano wire and ran them off camera, where he and two Japanese assistants would fire off the three arrows. He showed his assistants how the set-up worked, but they did not seem convinced that it was entirely safe.

"What if the wire breaks?" they asked anxiously.

"The arrow would just fall to the ground," said Dawson. "Look, I'll show you."

He took them behind the building, where no one was watching, and showed them how it worked. After two or three demonstrations, he was able to convince the assistants to try it. Dawson pulled back his bow and let the first arrow fly along the piano wire and smack into the pine. The first assistant stepped up and timidly let an arrow loose. It fluttered up to the target and bounced off.

"More power," said Dawson, and showed him again.

Finally he overcame the Japanese concern for the English actor's safety. But now the actor himself was being uncooperative. "He didn't want to be bothered doing it our way," says Dawson. "It didn't allow him to emote."

The piano wire technique was also used in the scene where Buntaro is sitting inside with Blackthorne and asks him if he remembers the left post on the porch outside. Blackthorne says yes, he does, and Buntaro whips out his bow and puts three arrows through the same tiny hole of the paper wall. All arrows are presumably to be found in the left post outside.

The piano wire worked fine; it was the actor who made the scene difficult. He was supposed to have had lessons in the use of the bow, but somehow he never got them. Whipping out a bow samurai style is at about the same level of difficulty as roping a steer cowboy style. It requires practice. When the time came to shoot the scene, the actor went through the motions, but it was obvious that he had never had the promised coaching. The Japanese assistant who was responsible for arranging the coaching protested that the scene was impossible, that it couldn't be done, that it was just unrealistic. Dawson tended to agree ("It was make-believe time, a little bit of Hollywood") while Richard Chamberlain was not so sure ("They can do some amazing things"). To finally get the scene on film required some clever cutting—close-up of Buntaro with bow in hand, close-up of Buntaro lining up his arrow, close-up of arrow zinging through the air—but no smooth sequence showing the whole action.

The scene in which Omi beheads a man for not bowing to him also struck some of the Japanese as unrealistic—not be-

Yuki Meguro knew how to handle his sword.

He was right on the mark.

cause of the way it was engineered, but because they felt that, since bowing is so automatic, no Japanese would have forgotten to bow. The hardest part of that scene from a special effects perspective was finding a mannequin to use for the man. The rest was easy.

At the prop shop, Dawson took a mold of the man's head. Then he hollowed out the inside of the mold, ran surgical tubing into it, and stuffed it with meat and 3-M blood. He attached the mold of the actor's head to the mannequin body and put rubber arms on the body to give the effect of movement. At the base of the mannequin's spine was a hinge, so he could bow, and running down his leg, under his costume, was a cable, so Dawson could control the movement from off camera.

He took the mannequin down to the beach, where the scene was to be shot, and affixed it to the ground. Then he gave Yuki Meguro, who played Omi, the sharpest samurai sword he could find and showed him the hairline on the neck where he had to chop. If he was more than a quarter inch off the mark, the mannequin would have to go back to the shop for repairs.

Meguro had made other samurai movies and knew how to handle his sword. The cameras rolled and Dawson started the mannequin bowing. Meguro raised his sword and brought it smoothly through the air. As he hit the neck, Dawson hit his button, and fake blood came squirting out through the surgical tubing in the mannequin's neck. They finished the scene in one take.

Bows and arrows—it almost sounds like a real Western Western. Not even horses were missing. But American riders found that horses were not quite the same in Japan. Blackthorne and Mariko were supposed to be riding swiftly through a field. The stuntwoman who was doubling for Mariko seemed to be having trouble with her horse. It was running away with her and, through three takes, almost bucking her off. In the fourth take, the American double for Blackthorne thought he would be gallant. As Mariko's horse started to run away again, he leaned over to grab it. The result? He fell off his own horse, got kicked in the ribs, and wound up in the hospital.

About the only special effect that came off trouble-free was Mariko's cremation. "That was a simple, controlled fire,"

explains Dawson. "They carry her in on an open palanquin and set her on top of four-feet-high logs. What I did there was run a bunch of copper tubing under the logs, connected to three tanks under pressure, and filled with a mixture of diesel fuel, gasoline, and benzoyl. On one of the logs facing the camera, where the two actors were going to set the fire, I soaked it with kerosene, so it would be a slow-starting fire, not just go into a big blaze. After it burned within reason for a time, I would open up the gas and give it a little bit more. You'd see just the flames licking at the bottom. Then, when that got believable, I opened up the diesel fuel and gas. In a matter of three minutes, you've got a roaring fire. And it just engulfs Mariko. Nothing out of the ordinary."

It sounded so easy in the script:

"A gaping fissure opens in the ground and rushes toward them at an incredible speed—Toranaga and Mariko teetering on the brink of the cleft. Blackthorne just stares, swallowed by his fear, incapable of thought or action. Then Toranaga starts to topple into the fissure. Blackthorne comes out of his stupor and lunges forward—pushing Mariko back from the edge and grabbing out for Toranaga ... The split earth is heaving violently, mud and rocks pouring down..."

And it might well have been easy—if it had never rained.

Bob Dawson's solution to staging the earthquake was ingenious. He found a two-acre field which already had natural fissures running in a zig-zag pattern, left by a previous rain. These fissures he widened into earthquake proportions—four feet wide and eight feet deep—so that when the time came for the earth to open up, tents and people would have plenty of room in which to be swallowed up.

Then he covered up the newly dug trenches with large sections of plywood, and covered the plywood with earth, so that the field looked just like new. The plywood was supported only by thin posts that were weakened about halfway down so that they could easily collapse. At the weak point of the post—called a "weak knee"—a small explosive was attached, which could be set off from a distance on cue. When the explosive went off and the weak knee collapsed, the plywood would come tumbling into the open trench with the earth on top. To the cameras, it would look for all the world like an earthquake.

In the space of two weeks, Dawson dug about 50 of these "earthquake faults," each supported only by a collapsible post. His explosives were attached to transition wires and the wires ran to his detonation board. It was all ready to go. But the film-makers were not. Because of a change in the shooting schedule, the earthquake would not be needed for a month. During that month, the rains came.

Six or seven cameras were set up all around the field the day before the earthquake was to be filmed. Once those explosives went off and the earthquake started, there would be no

Opposite page: Setting up the earthquake sequence.

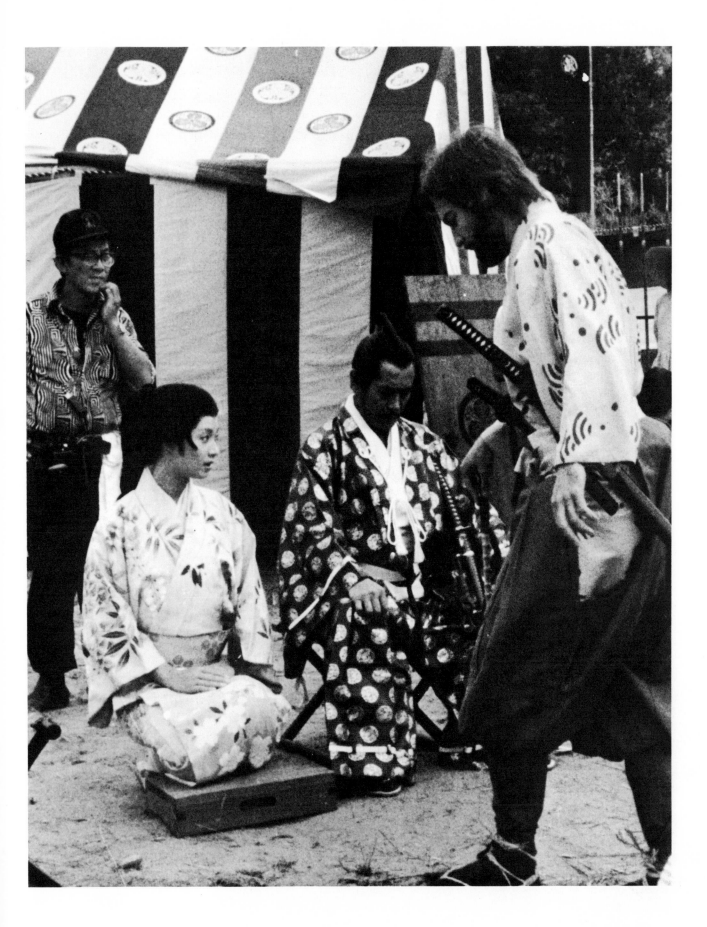

stopping it. If they didn't get it on film, they would never convince Bob Dawson to stage another.

That night it rained heavily. When the crew got out to the field in the morning, it was beautiful. To Dawson's eyes, though, it was anything *but* beautiful. He feared the worst for his explosives and weak knees, and went down to have a look. As he climbed into one of the trenches, under the plywood, he could see that there were two feet of mud underneath. If that mud had packed his posts, they would no longer collapse on cue. There was no way to tell without actually setting off the explosives, so he decided to gamble. If the first three posts collapsed, all the rest would fall like a stack of dominoes, and he'd have one earthquake in the can.

The rehearsals began. It was imperative that everyone know exactly what he had to do, where he had to be, and when he had to be there. All the shooting angles had to be lined up perfectly. All the cameras had to be doublechecked to be sure they were loaded with film and fresh batteries. The scene was to begin with a tent shaking and then collapsing. Actors would then run over, get caught in the earthquake, and go down into the faults. If an actor didn't get to the right place on time, he couldn't stop and do it over. "Just keep running," Dawson told them. "If the first fissure doesn't get you, the next one down the line will." It took about four hours to make sure everyone understood the scene. There would be no second chances.

The timing was down. The cameras were ready to go. "OK, action! One, two, three . . ." An explosion went off with a loud bang. Blackthorne and Mariko clung to each other, terrified, while the tent swayed back and forth. But nothing else happened. The ground did not open up. Dawson did not fire any more charges and waved to the director to call off the scene. Then he climbed down into the first trench to see what had happened. As he suspected, the mud had hardened around the post like concrete. Even though the explosive had gone off, it had not been able to loosen the post. But it was right on the verge of collapsing. Dawson figured as little as two pounds of pressure would do it.

"You might as well call lunch now," he told director London. "While people are eating, I'll get this fixed and ready

Opposite page:
"Just keep running,"
Dawson told them.

to go." His idea was to go back down into the trench and lay a "kicker" up against the weakest part of the post. The kicker would be another 2 × 4 wedged between the post and the side of the trench. An explosive would be attached to the kicker and when it went off, its force would knock the main post apart and everything would come tumbling down.

"I just want to take one man down with me," Dawson told his interpreter. "You stay on top so you can tell the other guys what size to cut the 2 × 4." He dug an emergency exit hole at one end of the trench, just in case, and a breathing hole at the other. Even with those it was still quite dark down there.

He would go into the trench with an assistant named Haga-san. Before they descended, he told Haga-san through an interpreter just what they were going to do. First they would measure, to see how long the kicker needed to be. Dawson would shout the measurement up to the interpreter. An assistant on top would cut the kicker to size, and pass it back down. Haga-san was to put it in place—*gently*—to see how it fit. If it was good, he was to make a fist. If it was not, he was to shake his head no. As usual, the conversation back and forth between Haga-san and the interpreter took much longer than it had taken Dawson to explain things in English.

They went to the first station, measured the kicker, got it in place, put the charge on. No problem. They went on to the next station, and a second Japanese assistant came down to help. Dawson was not sure if the second man had understood the instructions. The translation had been unusually quick. But they had only one more to go. He measured for the kicker, and called up his measurement to the interpreter. When it was cut, the second assistant went up to get it and bring it back down. The fit was a little snug, so Dawson sent it back up with instructions to take another quarter inch off.

"*Whoooops!*" said the second assistant, and the last thing Dawson saw was the assistant holding on to the main post and tugging at it.

"Let go of it!" shouted Dawson in English.

But by then it was too late. There was a loud *crack!* Dawson looked up and saw a 4 × 6 foot piece of plywood crashing down towards him. He threw his elbows out and held onto his knees as the plywood, covered with earth, landed with its full weight on his shoulders. Had he gone flat, the weight would have killed him. As it was, he wound up in a crouched position on his knees and elbows, with all the weight of the wood and earth on his back, and his mouth inches away from the oozing mud.

The second assistant had escaped through the first trench. Haga-san got out by the emergency exit. But when Dawson tried to move, he found he was pinned underground by the earth and plywood. Through the breathing hole, Haga-san climbed back into the trench. He found a 2 × 4 to help prop the weight and keep it from pressing Dawson's face any closer to the mud. Haga-san stationed himself there, holding the 2 × 4 with his hands.

Left:
Dawson examines a fissure.
Right:
Frankie Sakai and Maggie Dawson.
Bottom:
The Shinto priest landed a part in the film.

Meanwhile, pandemonium had broken loose on top. While Dawson had been working on the earthquake, the crew had gone to work on a different scene about 100 yards away. At the sound of the accident, they all came running over to see what had happened. But they did not understand how the earthquake had been constructed. They did not know that under the earth were the trenches and that the earth upon which they were all frantically gathering rested directly on Bob Dawson's back.

"Get these people off my back!" he shouted to the interpreter, and he meant the expression quite literally. "I'm sinking fast. You guys gotta get me out of here!"

Everyone was talking at once. The Japanese could not understand the Americans and the Americans could not under-

A rescue team took Dawson to the hospital.

stand the Japanese. The Japanese firemen and rescue team arrived, and no one could explain to them what had happened. They started running over the earthquake site—those fragile sections of plywood engineered specifically to collapse on a moment's notice—and they joined the crowd that was standing on Dawson's back.

Voices were raised. The firemen would not move out of the area and the American crew could not make them understand the danger they were creating not just for Dawson but for themselves. The wire services had gotten the news and besieged the area with helicopters and photographers. Finally one of the Americans kicked a Japanese fireman in the head to get him to move. Director of photography Andy Laszlo physically removed another. One of the news photographers kept coming back to the fissures, only to be thrown out again and to come back again, until one of the Japanese grips reared back and threw a fist at him.

Dawson's knees started to buckle, pushing his face closer and closer to the mud. The mud, inches from his nose, made it difficult to breathe. As slowly as he could, he filled his lungs with air. Then he had time only to shout to Haga-san, "Listen, you gotta get me out of here *quick!*" before he was out of breath again.

Andy Laszlo, the director of photography, bellowed for everybody to shut up. For the first time in more than half an hour, one person was going to take control and give directions. Between the grip truck and the Japanese rescue truck, Laszlo was able to get together a block and tackle.

He got a rope around the collapsed timber on Dawson's back. "No!" shouted Dawson with his last breath. "Those are the wrong boards! The nails are digging into my back!" Then he passed out.

Laszlo quickly readjusted the ropes. He knew he didn't have much time. As the block and tackle slowly raised the timber, the crowd waited anxiously. There lay Dawson, stretched out at the bottom of the trench. He was breathing with effort. A rescue team loaded him into an ambulance and took him to the hospital. There were no broken bones and he was back at work the next day.

Opposite page:
To the cameras, it
would look like
an earthquake.

Japanese labor law requires a thorough investigation any time an employee is injured. So, as soon as Dawson was through at the hospital, he had a lengthy appointment at the police station to make out a complete report on how it happened, why it happened, and what would prevent it from happening again. "We have investigations in this country, but not like that," says Dawson. "In the States, they don't shut the job down. They put a blanket over the guy and say, 'OK, let's go. Call down the hall, let's get another welder up here.' And that's it. But over there, it was a complete investigation. And I think that's good. Because they take a life there pretty seriously. They don't want to hurt *anybody*.

"They couldn't actually stop us from going ahead with it, when you came right down to it. But they *could* tell the crew that they didn't think they should go out there. That's all they would have had to hear, and they would have stayed home."

As it was, the Japanese would not come back to the set until they were completely reassured that the earth was not going to open up and swallow them all. They had a quite understandable premonition that, when the earthquake finally did go off, they would wind up under all that earth and plywood just as Dawson had. The crew explained that the trenches were so designed that the plywood and earth would sink into the ground first; it was physically impossible for anyone to wind up under it unless, for some reason, they had been crawling around down there as Dawson had.

But for the Japanese, the only real reassurance came when a Shinto priest arrived to bless the site. He walked out over the treacherous earthquake faults, businesslike and holy, and set up his altar. On the altar, he placed a candlestick, incense, and a bottle of sake, and then went into his ritual, wandering all over the earthquake site, sprinkling sake.

"Hey, wait a minute!" said producer Bercovici. "Shouldn't you stop him? He's walking right over the earthquake site."

"Are you kidding?" said Dawson. "How are we going to convince them that it's safe to go out there if we won't even let their priest walk on it? *I'm* not going out there to stop him. Let him do his thing. It'll hold him, don't worry about it."

The priest, in full regalia, walked calmly around the earth-covered timber and explosives, sprinkling his sake and chanting his blessings. When he was through, the Japanese crew resumed work wholeheartedly. And the priest had landed himself a part in the picture—presiding over Mariko's funeral.

‡ ‡ ‡

Thinking back on the time he spent underground in Japan, Dawson remembers one thing clearly.

"All I was thinking down there was, Jesus, this is a hell of a way to go. And the only reason I'm going is lack of communication."

Opposite page: Rescuing Toranaga.

Below: Rebuilding Blackthorne's house after the earthquake.

Opposite page:
The procession to
Yedo.

Left and below:
Toranaga meets
with Lord Zataki
and is ordered to
Osaka.

Above:
The Portugese-
Japanese dictionary.

Opposite page:
At the First
Bridge.

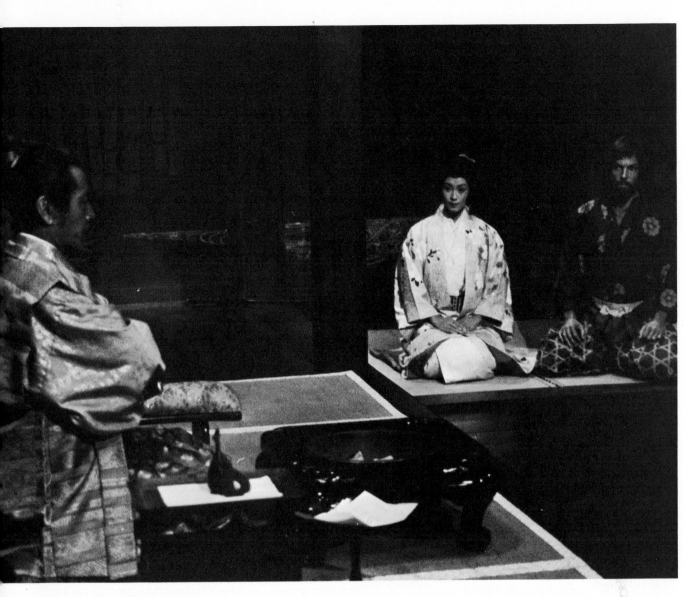

Opposite page, top: Omi and Kiku.

Opposite page, bottom: Rodrigues and Alvito discuss the Ingeles.

Above: Blackthorne requests a private audience with Toranaga.

Nagashima

The train sped by open farm land filled with rice fields, creeks, and rock formations. It stopped at every tiny town along the way, and even from the train it was clear that the people here were real country folks, leading a simple life. At a shoreline village surrounded by groves of orange trees, Eric Bercovici got out.

He looked out on the beautiful coves of Nagashima, one more enticing than the next, and wondered why, in a country that used every available inch of land, these coves had not been developed with luxury hotels. The area, as he saw it, was perfect for *something*. What he proposed to do here was build the major full-scale sets for *Shōgun*—a reconstruction of the Osaka waterfront plus the entire village of Anjiro.

In the cove, fishermen were placidly at work. It occurred to Bercovici that, when he returned later in the summer, these fishermen might get in the way of the water scenes he planned to shoot with the Erasmus and a Japanese galley. "Don't worry about that," he was told. "They will be long gone by the time you get here."

Still, he could not help but wonder how Nagashima had escaped the acquisitive clutches of the land developers. The mayor was actively courting *Shōgun*. He must have been interested in growth for his small town. And that's when Bercovici first heard about the typhoon that comes to Japan every year and always enters at the same spot, near Nagashima. "But don't worry," he was told. "It won't happen."

‡ ‡ ‡

Not long after, construction coordinator Al DeGaetano arrived in Nagashima, to find a town of 5,000 people in which everyone knew everyone else. Few Western tourists got this far, so DeGaetano and his crew were objects of some attention. Schoolchildren would follow them around the town, asking them for autographs, talking to them about the 16th century sailing ship that was anchored in one of the coves. As he got there, the spring rice crop was just being planted.

When he first went over to see the site Bercovici had selected for Anjiro, he had to climb down through the trees. There was no path down to the beach, much less a road. His first task, then, was to build a road, about 400 yards long, over which the crew could travel when they came later for filming. He had no idea, of course, what a Japanese road might cost. It came in for $15,000.

At the top of the road, he rigged a large water tank and a generator to feed water and electricity to the set below. Most of the camera equipment would be stored in the buildings of Anjiro and the waterfront, to avoid hauling it up and down that short but steep road. Four-wheel-drive vehicles would bring in the rest.

To construct the village of Anjiro, DeGaetano relied heavily on the Japanese art director, a well-informed man named Yoshinobu Nishioka. The houses were to be built with posted beams, thatched roofs, and Japanese tile. The two men sat down together to figure out what it might cost to build a 16th century Japanese village in 1979.

They laid out plans for three buildings, in different forms, and then, taking the square footage they had to work with, calculated how many houses they would need to fill the

First, a road.

village. They decided Anjiro would have a population of 26 houses. Then they started talking yen. DeGaetano totaled up the figures for what he thought it might cost. He asked Nishioka to do the same. Then they asked a Japanese foreman for *his* estimate. On an estimate that approached $200,000, the three of them showed only a $500 difference. DeGaetano wound up bringing his construction in under budget.

While a few key people came in from studios in Kyoto to help with the construction, much of it was done with the help of the locals—fishermen and middle-aged women. The workers would bring their lunches, often with portable hibachis to cook them on. It took about two months to finish the construction. At the same time, a Japanese contractor was hired to build the piers for the Osaka waterfront, bringing them in by sea at a cost of $80,000. That cost included removing the piers when the shooting was over.

DeGaetano was also responsible for taking care of the ocean-going vessels that would be used in the filming. The Golden Hinde, a copy of Sir Francis Drake's original, was on loan from its home port of San Francisco to play the part of the Erasmus, Blackthorne's ship. Captain Adrian Small, who sailed the ship from England to America in 1976 as part of the Bicentennial celebrations, took it from San Francisco to Yokohama in 55 days with a crew of 16 young men.

For *Shōgun*, the Golden Hinde would need some make-up. Despite its voyage across the Pacific, it did not look as beat-up as the Erasmus should have looked after challenging the straits of Magellan. First it was given some particularly ragged sails. Then for later scenes, it was spruced up with new paint, a job which took three days. And the Golden Hinde was also used for a frigate, disguised with special panels that went over its own fittings.

Above:
Anjiro was built
from scratch.

Opposite page:
The galley.

At a local shipyard, DeGaetano had a 14-ton Japanese galley built. The patriarch of the family business had been building ships for three generations. Now he was building them mostly from fiberglass. But when he saw a chance to get back to good old wooden ships, he was delighted. The authentic oars, sails, and anchor that graced the galley were his doing. It was a solid, sea-worthy vessel.

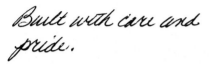
Built with care and
pride.

Shipbuilding in
Nagashima...

A solid, seaworthy
vessel.

Lifting the ship into the tank.

On July 12, 250 people descended upon Nagashima to begin filming. They stayed in the neighboring town of Owase, where the natives said it had been 20 years since they last saw a foreigner. By all reports, Owase outdid itself with hospitality and generosity. Americans would go out shopping for the afternoon and come back with 10 or 15 items the shopkeepers had given them—as gifts. American children who had come along with their working parents struck up a hot rivalry with the local baseball team. Some of the children even learned Japanese.

Many of the Americans had Japanese-style hotel rooms for the first time—tatami mats on the floor for sleeping, low tables for eating cross-legged. Not everyone was as adaptable as DeGaetano: "I would do lots of paperwork at night and in Tokyo I had a nice desk at the Imperial Hotel. Here, it was more difficult. But it was a real experience."

Shortly after their arrival, they realized that there had been a mix-up in the hotel accommodations. Here they were, commited to expensive sets already built in Nagashima, cut off from any supplies other than those they brought with them, three hours away from any other hotel, and they were being told that Owase's finest had been booked solid with vacationers for a Japanese holiday the first week in September. The shooting schedule called for them to finish in Nagashima mid-September.

Bercovici stormed back to his hotel room, ripped out his typewriter, and went to work on the script. For four hours he typed and scribbled, and when he was finished, he had come up with the solution. By simple revisions in the *Shōgun* script, he cut 10 days off the shooting schedule. Instead of leaving September 14, as scheduled, they would leave on the first.

‡ ‡ ‡

The first time the <u>Golden Hinde</u> and the Japanese galley appeared in the cove at Nagashima, it was obvious there would

It took thirty-six men to row the galley.

be problems. The only way the Golden Hinde could be moved was by sailing in the good old-fashioned way. The galley, even though it had just been built to *Shōgun's* specifications in the neighboring town, had no motor. The only way *it* could be moved was by rowing—and it took 36 oarsmen to do that.

After the first few days of shooting, there were film-makers in Nagashima who would not have minded taking that brand-new, solidly-constructed Japanese galley and chopping it into several thousand small pieces. On the water, it bobbed up and down like a cork. It would be stationed with great care in just the right place—the camera angles perfect, the sun casting just the right shadow, the background bright and beautiful. And then it would float away. Adjustments would be made. And it would float away again.

Mast, oars, sails, and anchor were authentic.

The Golden Hinde was not much better. It was a sea-going vessel, all right, just like Sir Francis Drake's. But Sir Francis and his crew must have gone through a lot of Dramamine. One of the assistant directors, a tall, thin man with a taste for sickly green shirts, was particularly sensitive to the ocean's rocking. On one of the roughest days at sea, he could be found lying on his back in the middle of the deck—the only place he could seek solace without getting in the way of the filming—and, his face matching the color of his shirt, barking his directions through a bull-horn.

One particularly tricky shot involved lining up the Japanese galley to run a convoy of ships blocking its path. Chamberlain was front and center in the scene, accompanied by 15 samurai armed with muskets. The samurai were to point their muskets straight at the camera and when Chamberlain, standing behind them, shouted "Now!" they were to fire.

In the water, it bobbed like a cork.

Since the whole ship was to appear in the scene, everyone but the camera operator was out on a raft next to the ship. Chamberlain leaned over the railing to consult with the director.

"When do I say 'Now'?" he needed to know.

But upon hearing the word "Now!" the Japanese actors started firing.

"No! No!" shouted the director.

The Japanese samurai, thinking he had shouted "Now! Now!", threw themselves into the firing with even more passion, until all their ammunition was gone.

And then there were the fishermen. It was time for the scene in which the Japanese galley arrives at Anjiro for the first time. The samurai were all lined up on the beach, waiting for the galley to appear. The Erasmus was anchored in the cove. London was on the galley with one camera. Bercovici was on the dock with another, hidden among the samurai. They were talking to each other over walkie-talkies, taking several hours to make sure everything was perfect. It was not a shot they wanted to repeat.

"OK, here we go," Bercovici heard over his radio. "I'm coming around the headlands. Roll the cameras!"

Thirty-six oarsmen strained at the oars. The samurai, in full dress, waited for their cues. With cameras whirring, the galley made its majestic appearance, first the mast, then the bow.

And then, right through the middle of the scene, came a 20th century fisherman in his motorboat. Very slowly. Putt. Putt. Putt.

"Sugiyama!" roared Bercovici. Sugiyama was in charge of directing water traffic. His was to become a familiar name in Nagashima during August, 1979. Frequently it could be heard resounding through the hills that hugged the shore. And it was always for the same reason. Fishermen. Those peaceful fishermen, whom Bercovici had seen when he first arrived in May and who he had been assured would be long gone by the time he was ready to film, were, on the contrary, out in force. Fishing, the primary industry of Nagashima, found its best-stocked waters in exactly the quiet cove where Bercovici had spent half a million dollars to construct Anjiro and the Osaka waterfront.

Opposite page:
It would be stationed with care...then it would float away.

And now the filming was interfering with the town's livelihood. The fishermen's union made it quite clear that their membership intended to continue their work there. They also managed to communicate the concept that a generous contribution to the union might persuade the members to take a few weeks off and fish elsewhere.

Thus it was that the fishermen's union of Nagashima, Japan, received a generous contribution from the coffers of *Shōgun*.

It was just another day in Nagashima. The galley was floating off course. The sun's angle was rapidly changing, making it difficult to match one shot with the next. The assistant director was seasick. And there was a Japanese fisherman parked in the middle of the scene. He was asked to leave, and politely complied, but in 45 minutes he was back again with his friends.

Meet the *non*-union fishermen of Nagashima. Were they not equally entitled to *Shōgun's* generosity? Whether or not they were entitled, each little visit to the cove was costing thousands of dollars. They got their donation.

‡   ‡   ‡

By that time, burning the ships was a suggestion that would have fallen on receptive ears. But, since the Golden Hinde did not belong to them, that was out of the question. The Erasmus does, of course, get burned in the course of the script, but somehow it just wasn't the same. A mock-up of the Erasmus' hull was constructed on the beach, and *that* was burned. As soon as the dailies came back from Kyoto, and it could be assured that the burning had been properly captured on film, the hull could be dismantled.

Those dailies from Kyoto were by this time turning into weeklies. They had to be driven to Kyoto, where the processing took a minimum of two days, and then driven back to Nagashima for viewing in a makeshift projection room. Orders were given to leave the burnt Erasmus standing until the dailies came back.

For some reason, Bercovici knew there would be a mix-up. The night they finished shooting the burnt Erasmus sequence, he went around to all of the production assistants personally to make sure they understood that they were *not* to strike the burnt <u>Erasmus</u> until the dailies check out. He tried to make it absolutely clear, to make sure no one could give the excuse, "Yeah, but I didn't know."

The next morning, the burnt <u>Erasmus</u> had been dismantled. Bercovici was furious.

"Who scrapped the burnt <u>Erasmus</u>?" he demanded.

Nobody knew.

"It didn't just get washed away. Who did it?"

Nobody knew.

"Who ordered it done?"

Nobody knew.

He called meetings. He sent memos around. He did everything he could to find out who had disobeyed his orders. And he never did find out.

When the film came back, it was fine.

The script called for 2,749 set-ups.

Above:
Eric Bercovici.

Right:
Joseph Jennings.

By the middle of August, as the rice was being harvested, it became clear that a typhoon was on the way. It would start to sweep in and then veer off. But everyone could feel that it was narrowing in on Nagashima.

On September 1, as Jerry London was finishing up the very last scene to be filmed in Nagashima, rain began to fall. Those few drops, which did not interfere with the scene, later turned into a typhoon that washed out roads and train tracks throughout Japan. In Nagashima, it rushed through the Anjiro and Osaka waterfront sets and left them useless.

It was then that Bercovici knew *Shōgun* would be completed on time. Despite the typhoon, despite the fishermen, despite the communication problems, despite the filming left to do in Kyoto, it would be completed. What if everything had gone smoothly and all the hotel accommodations had come through? They would have been stuck in Nagashima with two weeks' worth of filming left and no sets. The gods obviously had smiled upon *Shōgun*—or were they laughing?

While there were certainly similarities between Blackthorne and the Westerners who came to film his story 400 years later, the analogy only goes so far. Blackthorne did not know if he would ever be allowed to leave Japan. His survival depended upon his learning all he could about how the Japanese culture worked and how he could become a part of it.

The filmmakers, on the other hand, knew that they would be going home as soon as their work was done in Japan. Many of them were working so hard that they had no time to experience the Japanese world outside the studios even if they had wanted to. Many of them, like Blackthorne's crew, resisted Japan as long as they could.

Blackthorne and
his crew at Yedo.

"The Japanese were more mysterious when we left than when we arrived," muses *Shōgun's* associate producer Kerry Feltham. "We met one guy who had lived there for 11 years. He was 31 or 32, had gone there originally as a draft resistor, and spoke Japanese fluently. The Japanese were always astounded at his ability to speak conversational Japanese quickly and accurately. But he was sure that he had not in any serious way penetrated the Japanese culture himself and that he would go to his death, living there for the next 30 years, not understanding the Japanese. So what the rest of us did was just learn enough Japanese to get by at the supermarket or restaurant. There was no percentage in trying to become Japanese. We saw that and immediately gave up."

Many of the Americans stayed closed to the hotels, ate a lot of McDonald's hamburgers and Kentucky Fried Chicken—both of which do a thriving business in Japan—and frequented a bar in Kyoto called the Honky Tonk. The Honky Tonk's star attraction, outside of its watery Tequila Sunrise drinks, was a country and western singer with a Nashville drawl. His name, inlaid on his guitar with mother of pearl a la Merle Haggard, was Bo Yamamoto. Bo Yamamoto could sing perfect English, down to the drawl, but he couldn't speak a word.

Toranaga tests the loyalty of Lord Sudara by threatening to kill his children.

Left:
Outside Yedo Castle.

Below:
Blackthorne and
Vinck on the
Erasmus.

Opposite page:
Blackthorne arrives
at the Osaka Castle
gate—he is a
samurai.

"The Japanese were very interested in making a terrific cultural relationship with the Americans," says Jerry London. "But I must say that very few of them did. I'm as guilty as the next one, but I really didn't have time to do it. They wanted to have meetings. They loved to sit and talk over things. And we just wanted to *do*. Sure it would have been terrific to become culturally interwoven with the Japanese. But that's not what I was there for. I was there to make a movie, and it was an all-encompassing job. It was one of the shortcomings of the film, not really coming away with the whole company having great feelings of connection and communication. What we did come away with was a real taste of Japan and a great movie. I understand the culture, from reading the book. I just didn't have time to integrate myself into it."

The one person who did make a connection with the Japanese culture was Richard Chamberlain. And that was fitting: He was playing Blackthorne. Even those who identified more with Blackthorne's unhappy crew than with Blackthorne himself admired Chamberlain's ability to stay on an even upbeat keel through it all. "I don't think I heard him say one negative thing the whole time we were there," says Feltham. "He just floated along in what was probably a very Japanese kind of way, and enjoyed it all as much as he possibly could. He tried to understand as much as he could and formulate his character within himself as well as he could. He admired the culture and was very open."

Says Chamberlain, "I felt so sorry for a lot of the crew people there. They said, 'Here we are in the middle of Kyoto and there's nothing to do. I'm so tired of eating McDonald's hamburgers. There's nothing to eat.' And here they are in the midst of this immense treasure chest of the most beautiful, ancient culture, right there, seconds away. I used to jog around the Holiday Inn. Five minutes away were these wonderful temples. If you were there at the right time, you'd see incredible things. There was this one children's ceremony where the parents take their children to the temple to be blessed, and they all looked like little dolls in their traditional clothes."

‡ ‡ ‡

Hundreds of extras, all dressed as samurai, had assembled at the castle, waiting for shooting to begin. The

Japanese wardrobe man, a well-rounded scholar who worked in films just for fun, was unpacking Chamberlain's costume when he realized he had forgotten an obi—a long, brown sash that holds the swords and the costume together. He sent one of his assistants to get the obi, but it was several miles away, and in the meantime hundreds of extras were being paid thousands of dollars to wait around.

"I've got an idea," someone said. "Why not give him one of the extras' obis?" All the extras were wearing brown obis which would have done just fine for Chamberlain's garb. But the wardrobe man just sat there on a rock with his arms folded, looking perfectly miserable.

"It is my fault," he was saying in Japanese. "It is my fault. I take full responsibility. I messed up. I know it's my fault. I take responsibility."

"But look, man, we can get this done," said one of the Americans. "It's just one of those things. We'll get it done, no problem."

"It is my responsibility." He sat motionless on the rock. And he would not go back to work until he had completed his painful apology.

Another day they were filming a riding scene. In Japan, saddles are pointed in the middle. Chamberlain found them extremely uncomfortable and was on and off his horse all day long. Yoko Shimada, however, never got off hers. Finally, at the end of the day, he caught her wincing involuntarily.

"Yoko, don't you want to get down?" he asked.

"Oh, yes!"

So he arranged for her to get down. But even then she would not dismount alone or make herself comfortable without his interjection.

"She was in terrible pain," says Chamberlain, "but she wouldn't say it. It's kind of unmannerly to say you're in pain. You don't complain there. You just don't throw tantrums or get temperamental. They are at times incredibly inscrutable, mysterious people to the Western mind. You just *cannot* fathom them. Why they think a little matter of face is more important than getting the job done, I don't know. Our faces heal quickly. Theirs don't. I lost face a million times over there and it doesn't matter to me. But to them it matters a lot.

Opposite page: Entering the Great Hall.

"Any improvisation, any change of course, drives them to a total standstill. Somebody says, 'Wait a minute. She'd look better in red.' Or, 'We need to move the wall six inches this way.' These are little things that happen all the time in filmmaking. But if it wasn't written down beforehand, if they weren't prepared for it, it's another loss of face. And they worry that to death. They won't move. They break down. It's like a computer breakdown."

Despite the obstacles of culture and communication, some connections *were* made. Correspondences now flourish between Japan and Hollywood. Visits have been exchanged. Some of the crew even fell in love and brought Japanese companions home.

At the closing day party, several previously reticent Jap-

Mariko, prepared to commit seppuku.

anese approached Chamberlain to hug him or take his hand and tell him—in Japanese *and* in English—how much they had enjoyed working with him. "It was a flood of tremendous genuine good feeling," says Chamberlain, "and I'm sensitive to that. They had never expressed it to any large degree during the filming. I didn't even know a lot of them spoke English. There had been this distance. And I was so moved to find that they had been fond of me—and also so disappointed that I hadn't known earlier so that we could have made friends."

James Clavell, who was in Japan only for the first few weeks of filming, feels that, while certain difficulties could have been avoided, much of it was inevitable. "Films are not constructed by tolerance. Because tolerance requires patience. Patience requires time. And in our business, there is no time.

Onlookers at Mariko's seppuku scene.

When it's $100 a minute, everybody gets terribly nervous. Within the framework of what went on, it was a positive experience for everyone. It will not be forgotten easily."

How much of the misunderstanding could have been avoided? "I don't know," answers Chamberlain, "because I don't know anything about Japanese business. But the obvious thing would have been to have somebody from the start, who knew the ways of Japan, to get things organized. Someone who knew how the Japanese mind works, who knew they can't say 'no,' who knew when they were saying 'yes' when they really meant 'no.' I suppose people like that are hard to find. However, if I were going to spend $22 million, I think I could find one."

‡ ‡ ‡

The Western mind is accustomed to explanations. If you plug in A and B, you get C. If a catering truck will not come down from Ikuta, there must be a reason. And, in fact, there were reasons and explanations. But to understand them required relinquishing some preconceptions.

Chiho Adachi, 26-year-old bilingual secretary to James Clavell, was in a position to understand both cultures. The daughter of a high-ranking Japanese businessman, she was born in Japan and came to the States with her family at the age of five. From age 12 to 22 she lived in Japan, and then her father was assigned once again to the United States. As a result, she grew up at home in both cultures and in neither.

In Japan, with *Shōgun*, she felt so torn between the two cultures that she felt it would be better not to involve herself in straightening out the communications. Reflecting on what happened there, she feels that more understanding of how the Japanese communicate with each other would have been of great help to the Americans.

"If you tell someone to do something, they will eventually do it. And you will wait for it. You don't push. Unless it really becomes serious. And then when you do, you do it in a way that the other person will not be hurt and will not lose face. You don't just say, 'Hey, we're waiting. We have to get it done right now.' You have to say, 'Well, I know you're busy and I know you have a lot on your mind, but could you please do it, because we *are* rushing right now?' You have to go about it that way. That's how we get things done.

Opposite page: Ninja attack at Osaka Castle.

Opposite page:
Mariko is killed in
the Ninja attack.

Above:
Blackthorne discovers
Mariko's body.

Left:
The door burns for
the cameras, actors
safely out of range.

"I tried to explain it to people, and they did understand. But the frustration of not getting something done when they wanted it or not getting an answer when they wanted it was just too much for some people and they would go back to doing their own thing. People who were very gentle, mild-mannered people over here became so frustrated in Japan that we heard them yell, we heard them shout, we heard them pounding on desks. If I was translating, I would say, 'I am not going to translate if you're going to scream and yell like that. I cannot do it.' And I would just turn the other way and wait for him to calm down. Because the Japanese people will *not* take yelling and screaming. If you do that they will say, 'Look at this person who has lost control of himself and is yelling and screaming like that,' and they will lose complete respect for that person."

Bercovici and others were immensely frustrated by what they felt was an inability to get a straight "yes" or "no" answer from their Japanese associates. "You have to understand the Japanese mentality," says Adachi. "The Americans always ask for a 'yes' or 'no' answer. They want an answer on the spot. But the Japanese don't do it that way. They go in a kind of roundabout way. 'I will think about it' or 'It's a good idea.' The Americans didn't know how to interpret that."

One of the greatest misunderstandings involved customs regulations. In the last three weeks of shooting, the Americans discovered that Japanese law required them to take their film out of the country with sound and picture separated. Since June they had been rolling up the film with the sound and picture together—almost 75,000 feet of it.

A meeting was arranged with the customs officials.

"Is there anything specific that we should be doing here that we are not doing in order to comply with your regulations?" the Americans asked.

As usual, the question took about three minutes to make its way around the table. When it was fully translated, there was no answer from the customs officials. The Americans tried a more specific tack.

"May we take these out with the sound and picture rolled up together?"

"Ohhhhhh, no. No, you can't do that."

This went on for several hours, with the Americans trying to nail down every detail and imagine every catch they might be overlooking. "It was difficult to penetrate the truth of what was going on," says Feltham. "Unless you were very, very specific with your questions, you would be misled. Not necessarily intentionally. They simply wouldn't answer."

They ended up separating the track for several hundred thousand feet of film, a task that took six assistants four weeks working full-time. Had they known at the beginning, they would have separated the film as they went along.

"In Japan you have to ask the right questions," explains Adachi. "If you ask just *anybody*, they will give you part of the answer, but if you don't pursue them—'Is that all? Is there any more?'—if you don't keep on asking that way, they will not give you the full answer. Because, you see, the Japanese think that you already know. If they told you, even though you already knew it, they would be shaming you, embarassing you. So if you really don't know something, you have to ask questions—to the right person at the right time—and that's what they were not doing.

"They'd say, 'How do you take this film out?'

"And the Japanese customs people would say, 'Well, you must fill in these papers.' But then they also assume that you know that you have to separate the sound and the picture. But they don't say it, because that would be disrespectful.

"If the Americans had bothered to say, 'In what condition should it be?' If they had asked *that* question, then they would have gotten the answer that it should be separated. You *have* to ask questions."

Why didn't the interpreters come to the aid of the Americans? They, presumably, knew what the right questions were and why no one was getting answers. "When an interpreter interprets, she should *only* interpret. To start asking questions on her own is, in some ways, an intrusion on the person she is working for. As a Japanese interpreter, she doesn't want to embarass her boss by starting to ask questions like that, when he's not even asking."

The same thing happened with the catering truck, when Bercovici expected a Western-style straight answer on why it could not be moved from Ikuta to Toho in time for lunch. Again, it was a matter of asking the right questions. It's a little like talking to a computer—if you don't ask for exactly the information you want or tell it exactly what you want it to do, you can get into big trouble.

But there was also a simple explanation for why the catering truck could not be moved. In Japan, permission from the motor vehicle department is required before a vehicle of that size can be moved. The caterers had already arranged their papers for a day at Ikuta. When they were told on short notice to move to Tokyo, there was no time to get the motor vehicle department's approval.

"Why didn't they tell that to Bercovici?"

Why didn't they tell that to Bercovici? Because he did not ask. "In the film, Brother Michael says to Blackthorne that the Japanese are a very predictable people," recalls Adachi, "and that something unpredictable is very hard for them to understand. They are completely thrown by it. So when things like that do happen, the Japanese have a tendency to say, 'Wait. We can't do it. We just can't do it.' And they won't even try sometimes, because they don't want to break the rhythm or the pattern that they have already set up. The Japanese are a very patient, tolerant people in that sense. If it can't be done, it can't be done. They won't get that upset about it."

Put in the same position, the Japanese would have simply eaten cold sandwiches and forgotten about it.

The premature dismantling of the burnt Erasmus was another incident in which the American way of doing things offended Japanese sensibilities. "The Japanese supervisor knew who did it. But he did not want the blame on the guy. Finally, he started saying, 'Well, I will take the responsibility.' The superior covers up for the people who are working for him.

"In Japan, heads do roll, but the wrong heads. If someone makes a mistake, he is not going to be blamed for it. It will be the person above him or the person above that person who will take the blame, and his head will roll. Because he is supposed to be supervising and if he does not do it well, he takes responsibility. In Japan, you very rarely fire a person. You just give him another job that does not have that much responsibility. In Japan, when you join a company, you stay there for the rest of your life, and you know that you will be taken care of for the rest of your life. Anything else would be betrayal. All this loss of face and shame and resentment is still there."

The Americans were making a film that dealt with those Japanese concepts—loss of face, shame, resentment. But it never occurred to them that the subject matter of their film also applied to the way they went about making the film. As Adachi explained, to simply give someone an order is disrespectful; it must be said in a way that preserves his dignity. So the curt orders that American directors give without thinking twice— "move to the left," "more emotion," "that's no good; let's do it again"—sounded harsh to Japanese ears.

Jerry London directs
Shimada and
Mifune.

Mifune, according to Adachi, was upset at being asked to retake scenes without being given an explanation. His assistant was constantly asking London, "What was wrong with it? I have to tell Mifune." And Mifune would be the one to take over direction of the extras when London could not get his ideas across through the interpreters. London might tell them, "Act impatient now. Act like there's something going on." And Mifune would step in to give them more specific directions on how to play the scene.

The Japanese crew also expected to be treated with more respect. One of the Americans had been in Japan just after the war, when Japanese filmmaking was in its infancy. At that time, the Americans were in the role of teachers. "I think he still had the same image 30 years later," says Adachi. "We're going to Japan again to teach these people how to make a film. And he influenced the rest of the crew. It was like, 'We're going to be the teachers and they're going to learn, and we're going to do it *our* way.' But, as you know, Japan has come up in the world since then. They have their own ways, and they are *set* ways. It was hard for them to accept that here are these Americans coming in and ordering them around and if they said anything, the Americans would just reject it. It didn't matter if the result was the same. It had to be done in an American way.

"If they had explained to them what they wanted and given the Japanese time to do it their way, it could have been done with the same result. But the Americans were complaining, 'They don't know how to do *anything*. They don't know how to paint. They don't know how to make a set. The lighting is bad. The facilities are bad.' But the Japanese have been making good movies with this equipment and technique, and they should have been given more credit for that. With the pressure that they had to make a movie in a certain set time limit, I guess they didn't have time for that. In the small departments, everything went well. They had communication. One American with a group of Japanese did very well. The problems started when you put it all together."

The Westerners may not have understood Japan, but the Japanese seem to have understood the West. "Oh, definitely," says Adachi. "That's why, until 150 years ago, we had no communication or connection with the outside world. Since then, the Japanese have always had the feeling that they are late in doing things, that they are backwards. The urge to understand and know everything about the world has been so great for them that they study it very closely. They go to other countries and look at everything. The Japanese know Bob Dylan better than most Americans. They have to know about the outside world so they can catch up with it. The Americans, being a strong country, don't have to look outside. They can just be interested in themselves. The Japanese can't do that."

The mores of *Shōgun*—honor, shame, loss of face—still speak to the modern Japanese mentality. So the film, even though it will not strike the Japanese as a strict rendering of their familiar history, can still be accepted as a fictional romance. "There is still that traditional side within everyone," says Adachi. "Even *I* have problems with it. But they took so much trouble telling the Americans how things should be done to keep it authentic that in the end everyone felt they had had a role in an important project."

A Gift to Japan

On the eve of battle, Toranaga sits meditatively at the crest of a hill. Tomorrow, 40,000 warriors will die to make him Shōgun. But today he watches, as the first Englishman to arrive in his country starts work on a new sailing ship. Toranaga knows he must destroy the second ship as he destroyed the first, for Blackthorne is too valuable to him. For the moment, though, Blackthorne is blissful in his ignorance. He is vigorous and fulfilled—and not only by his dreams of the future. Blackthorne the Westerner has made a life for himself in the East as well.

What would happen if Blackthorne ever made it home? Surely he would be ecstatic to see his own land again. But might he, after the initial emotion had faded, start to dream of the Orient again?

Tomorrow, Shōgun.

Bob Dawson's wife, Maggie, knew some of those film-makers who couldn't wait to get home. They dreamt of painting the house and getting out the barbeque. They were the ones who were tired of Japan. But now she hears them singing a different tune.

"I want to go back," said one of her friends.

"But I thought you didn't like it."

"Well, I didn't think I did. But now I realize that I was wrong."

"I'd *love* to go back," says Mrs. Dawson. "Any day. I think my favorite part was all the time I had in Japan with no pressure. I felt so relaxed. I don't know if it was because I was an outsider there, but I don't think so. They have a happy feeling. They make you happy. When I got back here I felt the pressure right away. Sure, I was homesick there at first. But now that I'm back, I'm homesick for Japan."

"I don't think people realize how different the Japanese are from us," says Chuy Elizondo, "even though when you get to Tokyo it's a big city just like Los Angeles or New York. But after that experience, I think a lot of the Japanese. They are very honest, very clean. I think we have a lot to learn from them."

Back home in December, the work had just begun. Five hundred thousand feet of film were printed, out of a total 750,000 feet shot. Ninety hours of film had to be edited down to 12—selecting the right camera angles from the various that had been shot, blending the sequences, timing it all to the second. Four editors, each assigned a different section, took over a large portion of the post-production facilities on the Paramount lot in Hollywood, working through the summer, finishing shortly before *Shōgun* was due to air on NBC.

Three sound effects specialists worked full-time putting in explosions, footsteps on gravel or sand, and the sound of arrows flying through the air. Composer Maurice Jarre worked on the music. Until he could finish his score, temporary background music was sandwiched in from the music library at Paramount. In April, any sound problems in the original track would be repaired. Dubbing of sound, music, and dialogue would be finished by August, so August could be spent at the film lab, checking the prints.

At the same time, a two-and-a-half-hour version of *Shōgun* was being edited—the version that would be shown in theaters abroad and perhaps eventually in the United States. The theatrical version had its own script and was shot at the same time as the 12-hour version. It is, of necessity, an abbreviated version and, in some ways, a different story. Many of the characters—some of the priests and all of the crew—are eliminated, to center on three main characters: Blackthorne, Mariko, and Toranaga. Director London sees it basically as a love story. He shot different scenes for it, some featuring more nudity and violence than was appropriate for television.

And the Japanese came over to edit a theatrical version for showing in Japan, a film that is being promoted side-by-side with Kurosawa's latest. While the American version centered on Blackthorne and assumed that the Japanese dialogue would be unintelligible to the audience, the Japanese version obviously had to take a different approach. They had a considerable amount of footage to work with, featuring some of their finest actors speaking in their own language. In their version, the scenes filmed in Japanese are given more importance than in the English version.

The Japanese version gave *Shōgun* an interesting twist. The original goal of Bercovici's script was to change the point of view of the novel, making the audience see everything through Blackthorne's eyes. Blackthorne was the hero; Japan was the

Above:
Yabu, Lady Kiri,
and Blackthorne
at Mariko's
funeral.

Right:
Brother Michael
looks on as a
doctor bandages
Blackthorne's eyes.

Opposite page:
Dell'Aqua intervenes
as Ferriera
prepares to fire at
Blackthorne.

alien world. Now, the Japanese editors took that material and restructured it, down-playing the scenes that are in English and emphasizing the scenes that the Japanese audience will understand. From the same script, they came up with a film that changed the point of view once again, showing Blackthorne's story from the Japanese perspective, making Blackthorne the alien.

Even the 12-hour television version must naturally leave out much of the novel's intrigue and detail. To include everything, says London, would have taken another five or six hours. "Clavell wrote a very intricate, complicated political novel, which was wonderful. What Eric [Bercovici] tried to do was simplify as much as he could in the screenplay. And I tried to keep it to an understandable level for the audience. People have said that the mini-series as presented is easier to understand than the book. And that's probably true."

How will the Japanese react to this American version of their national history? "I'm not Japanese, so I can't tell you it's a film the Japanese will love," London says. "The Japanese, if they're super-critics, may find faults in the cultural presentation, but they won't find any in the story. We went to great lengths to make it accurate. But you must remember that the film was not made for the Japanese. It was made for the English-speaking world, as entertainment. I'm not sure how the Japanese will accept it, but I do know that they like films that are romantic and full of adventure and action, and this picture has it. And it also shows their beautiful country."

If *Shōgun* were a 12-hour film about modern Tokyo made by Americans for American television, no one would be thinking of it as a Japanese film. But because this was perhaps the first time foreigners had gone to Japan to make a Japanese costume film, a period piece, and because they used Japanese actors, filmmakers, and facilities, there is a tendency to forget that it is still, in the end, an American production.

"We brought television a long way," beams London. "Everybody's saying this is too good for television. I compare it to the highest piece of entertainment, in the classical sense of the word, that has been done on television. It's not *Roots. Roots* was a biographical drama with fine acting. Ours is an adven-

Opposite page: Yabu commits seppuku.

ture drama with fine acting. For me, it's closer to a public broadcasting program like *I, Claudius*. We have the advantage of doing it on film instead of tape and having it out in the open and traveling."

Clavell, too, is pleased with the screen version of his best-seller. "Whatever happens, I am content to assume the responsibility," he says. "*Shōgun* in novel form and film form is the best I can do at this moment in time—with heaven as it is."

And *Shōgun* abounds with Clavell's admiration for Japan. "For me, Japan is always rare, unique. Japan and Japanese have a very special place in my firmament. As of right now I'm *taisetsu na hito*, a Very Important Person, as far as they're concerned. Because if *Shōgun* is publicized correctly and is shown correctly on television, it will make history as far as the television medium is concerned. I believe that it will turn America's eyes—for how long, I don't know—Eastwards, where they *should* be. Because if we can't learn from the Japanese and the Chinese, the Asian people, we are buggered. Right now, we're losing."

As for what a Westerner, however well-informed, can show the Japanese about their own history, Clavell begs their indulgence. "I would petition Japanese audiences to lend me their minds for a few hours, to compartmentalize what they have been taught about their legendary past and allow me to show them a *gai-jin's*, a foreigner's story about an Englishman who came to Japan in 1600 and was made a samurai by the Lord of the Kwanto, who fell in love with an incredible, high-born Japanese lady, to lose her tragically when she died protecting her liege lord."

And for American audiences, Clavell hopes *Shōgun* will stimulate interest in a culture that has much wisdom to share with us. "*Shōgun* was written, hopefully, to be a bridge between East and West and to dramatize and try to explain the Land of the Gods to the West. It is passionately pro-Japanese and brought together with loving care. In a way, it is my gift to Japan."